BANGKOK
THEN AND NOW

STEVE VAN BEEK

To Linda & Arnold,
Hope the new millennium
finds you in this great city.
Best wishes.
Steve

AB PUBLICATIONS

Bangkok Then and Now

Published by AB Publications
163/19 Baan Chollada Soi 14, Bang Bua Thong
Nonthaburi 11110, Thailand

Editorial Consultant: Dr. Nid Hinshiranan
Assistant Editor: Orawan Sriudom
Text Editor: Richard Lair
Editorial Assistant: Savika Srisawat
Proofreader: Cora Sukhyanga

Designer, Layout: Jeithaval Phasookhush
Design Concept: Thongchai Nawawat
Maps: Preechai Praisawasdi
Production Co-ordination: Ramesh Shrestha

With grateful thanks to:
Anake Nawigamune, Ariya Sintujarivatr, Sean Brady, M.R. Butri Viravaidya,
Jon Harger, George Hooker, Barry Owen, Davis Pike, Pow Kham-Ourai,
Pratoom Suwanalot, Julian Spindler, Tak Thitibanna, Dr. Virachai na Nakorn,
and especially to Dr. Nid Hinshiranan for his deep knowledge of Bangkok.

The author thanks the dozens of kind people who took the time to walk a
strange *farang* hundreds of meters to identify the site of an old photograph.
And especially to those citizens who took him under their wings, opening their
doors and rooftops — even locating ladders — caught up in the spirit of
preserving some of the city's past.

*Cover photograph: The Grand Palace as seen from Thonburi, two views
taken one hundred years apart.*

Printed in Bangkok, Thailand by Phongwarin Printing

ISBN Number: 974-87063-9-7

CONTENTS

Introduction: Yesterday, Today   10

Bangkok at the End of the Nineteenth Century   15
Two Centuries, Two Cities   16
Bangkok's Geometry   26
      Rajdamnern Avenue in the Year 1900   42
Street Life   46
The Imprint of its Inhabitants   48
Municipal Services   54
      Trams, a Way of Life   58

Living in Bangkok at the Beginning
      of the Twentieth Century   63
Our Window on an Antique Age   65
The European Quarter   71
Lifestyles   77
Fears and Concerns   85
      Police Blotter for 1900, 1901   94
      Bangkok's Residences for Miscreants   96
Recreation   99
      An Evening on the River   106
Getting Away   110
      Wild Wild East   112
Looking Homeward After Years Away   114
      Home Leave   115

Bangkok on the Cusp of the Third Millennium   116
Bangkok 2000   118
      Grappling with Jams   124

      Map of Bangkok 1901   126
      Map of Bangkok 1999   128

FOREWORD

The stereoscope was invented in the 19th century as a novel way to lend perspective to photographs. Two identical photos taken from slightly offset lenses and then placed side by side in the stereoscope gave the viewer a three-dimensional image of a scene which a single photograph could not convey.

Similarly, this book has adopted a stereoscopic vantage point to portray the changes occuring over a century. Placing a photograph taken on the eve of the 20th century next to one taken at its end, vividly communicates a sense of the dynamic changes — and the enduring elements — that Bangkok has experienced.

Most of the photographs are from the National Archives. Unfortunately, the backs of most of the pictures contain but brief pencilled commentary and educated guesses as to subject and location; rarely is the date noted. For the author, the attempt to identify the locale in order to take a matching photo often turned into a detective hunt, trudging through Bangkok's labyrinthine streets and lanes for hours until landmarks began to emerge that matched those in the photos. A frequent reward was the discovery of a neighborhood he hadn't known existed or a chance encounter with Thais who became intrigued by the search and joined in. More often than not, hours of perspiration were rewarded with a triumphal "Ah-ha!" as what had been an obscure photo sprang to life as a reflection of the great city's past. Sadly, many of the photos could not be identified and must remain in the storage cabinet to await the day when a serendipitous stroll through a new district triggers a memory of it.

Another key element of the book are the news items from the *Bangkok Times* of 1900 and 1901. On an idle afternoon in the Siam Society library in 1979, I stumbled across bound volumes — which, alas, have since crumbled to dust — which fascinated me for what they said about an epoch, and told us about ourselves. I eventually scoured every page of every edition for those two years, selecting the most intriguing stories, typing them on a broken-down typewriter, and offering them to the readers of the *Bangkok Post* in a fortnightly column called '1900', and '1901'. I'd always believed the stories deserved a more permanent place in local lore and thus had squirreled them away for 20 years until conceiving the idea for this book. For me, they poignantly supplement the photos, giving an added dimension to the histories of the end of the 1800s, one not found in most books.

This book is by no means a complete history of Bangkok. Vast amounts of printed sources and photographs survive but that material reveals two vastly different perceptions. While the Thai writings and photographs deal mostly with people — notably the royal court — the foreigners were intrigued by things and by places. Thus, this book essentially reflects a European perception of Bangkok, echoing Western sensibilities and pre-occupations at the dawn of a new century.

Note: Throughout the book, small maps serve as guides for explorations of the city. The number in the circle refers to the page on which the photo appears. The arrow indicates the direction the photographer was facing.

This view looking north from the top of Phu Khao Thong (the Golden Mount) down to Pan Fah, dates from the 1880s: outer Rajdamnern Avenue was constructed in 1900. At this point, Klong Banglampoo, dug in 1783 by 5,000 Laotien war prisoners, is crossed by a small wooden bridge and the only familiar landmark is Mahakan fortress on the city wall at left. It is recorded that when King Chulalongkorn tried to cruise down Klong Banglampoo to Wat Saket for a Krathin ceremony, the bridge had to be removed to make way for the Royal Barge. Designed by Italian engineers, the brick and cement bridge appeared at the end of Chulalongkorn's reign, and was widened in 1957. The Dynastic Chronicles for Rama I's reign note that Klong Mahanak—seen branching off to the right—was excavated as "a place where the people could go boating and singing and reciting poems during the high-water season, just like the customs observed in the former capital at Ayutthaya." By 1900, it would be the scene of a lively Floating Market.

Introduction
YESTERDAY, TODAY

A.D. 1900 to A.D. 2000. Only one hundred years and the merest blip in the span of geologic time, yet the century has been witness to change more dramatic than any in Thailand's history, altering Bangkok's face forever.

In 1900, Thailand was an agrarian society, comprising concentric circles of habitation defined by the lush surrounding vegetation. Villages and towns were dots embraced by vast fields of

Sunday morning golf is quite an institution now in Bangkok. Play begins about 7 a.m...and goes on till noon or later. Members take turns to provide refreshments, much needed and well earned and there is a goodly number of 'dead men' piled up at the end of the morning.

The Clubhouse is a Sala [pavilion] in front of the Museum [at Sanam Luang]. On average about twenty turn up and although a rival attraction is threatened — we refer, of course, to the hunting of the snipe bird — the golfing fraternity has considerable faith in the devotion of its followers.

—July 1901

Sanam Luang is virtually unchanged today except that the view of Wat Phra Kaew is now obscured by tall tamarind trees.

vibrant green rice, the fields in turn enfolded by the darker green rainforests still inhabited by hunters and gatherers. The largest dot was Bangkok, the nation's commercial core and an urban island in an endless sea of rice paddies veined by canals.

In truth, 'dot' describes 19th century Bangkok less accurately than 'line'. The city's evolution mirrored its rural roots, following the ribbon pattern of settlement whereby most of the populace clung to the banks of the nurturing Chao Phya River.

The mighty Chao Phya was the nation's liquid road to northern towns such as Chiang Mai, reached by a six-week boat journey. The river was also Thailand's highway to the world; ships with foreign names adorning their sterns sailed it on their way to and from distant ports, dropping anchor off the city's quays and wharves. A century ago, not a single bridge spanned the river. The first, the Rama VI Bridge, would not be constructed until 1926, and not for vehicular or pedestrian traffic but for trains traveling down the southern peninsula to Singapore.

A noble couple pose in a studio, their costume suggesting the photo was taken during the reign of King Vajiravudh who ruled from 1910 to 1925.

Until the 16th century, there was no Bangkok, only Thonburi. The Chao Phya River flowed along a course now defined by Klong Bangkok Noi and Klong Bangkok Yai. To shorten the travel time between the sea and the capital at Ayutthaya, King Chairajathiraj (reigned 1534-1546) ordered that a two-kilometer canal be dug across the river's neck from a point now marked by the Bangkok Noi Railway Station to one near Wat Arun. Erosion ultimately widened the channel to become the river we know today.

Thonburi (Money Burg) was a sentinel town with fortresses on both sides of the river — the one at the mouth of Klong Bangkok Yai still exists — to guard against invasion from the sea. As Thonburi was also Ayutthaya's customs port, many Thais settled there and it soon grew into a small city. After Ayutthaya's destruction by the Burmese in 1767, King Taksin (1767-1782) moved his palace to Thonburi's safe haven in the vicinity of Wat Arun.

At that point, Bangkok was little more than a village. It began to grow only after King Rama I established it as the seat of his new dynasty in 1782. During most of the 19th century, Bangkok was the center of royal power and commerce, and the home of the Chinese and

The standard of beauty and fashion during King Mongkut's reign (1851-1868)—with the cropped hair women had worn since the Ayuthaya period— demonstrates how dramatically things had changed after King Chulalongkorn encouraged women to dress in European-style, wearing their hair long.

European communities. The bulk of the Siamese population continued to reside on the river's western bank which would remain essentially rural until the opening of the Phra Buddha Yod Fah Bridge (Memorial Bridge) in 1932.

The city of Bangkok was defined by water. Crisscrossed not by streets, but rather by dozens of canals; transportation was primarily by boats of which there were dozens of types suited to their purpose.

The most prominent, the sampan (literally, 'three boards', to describe its construction), carried passengers, hawkers, even entire restaurants from door to door. Most city roads were dirt tracks; in 1900 Bangkok's first paved street was less than 40 years old. Although the first automobile made its appearance in 1897 — purchased by a noble, Chao Phya Surasakh Montri — it was horse-drawn gharries, Victoria Brougham carriages and trams that carried people through the streets. Oxcarts ambled along city lanes and horse-pulled taxis trolled for fares

Once a scene of royal activity, the Royal Landing at Tha Chang Wang Luang is rarely used these days. Its decline in importance underscores the rise in importance of cars and roads. Wat Cheng, better known as Wat Arun, stands just as majestically now as it did then, unchallenged by the taller buildings that tower over many old monuments.

along the main thoroughfares, while rickshaws raced from one end of town to the other.

On their journey through the city, travelers threaded a jumble of buildings — most of them built of wood — that hugged the ground. Few residential or commercial buildings rose higher than three stories and *wat* (temple) roofs were still the tallest structures on the skyline — 398 of them in 1908, according to contemporary count — creating a veritable mountain range of sharp peaks.

The closest thing to factories were cottage industries, home businesses that manufactured wares to sell in their neighborhoods. Although numerous rice mills and sawmills lay along the riverbanks,

even as late as 1913, only six industrial companies were registered in all of Thailand. Agriculture was still the basic component of the economy, the abundant rice fields generating the wealth to buy imported goods.

Flash forward to A.D. 2000. Like a juggernaut, modern Bangkok has buried the paddy fields that once hemmed it. The primate city is now the locus of a galaxy of satellite cities, each with its

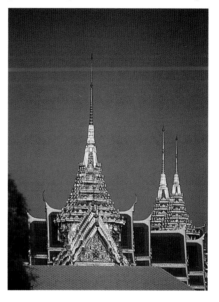

Above: Seemingly eternal, and reminiscent of the glory of heaven are the three spires of the Grand Palace. Left: A remembrance of days before automobiles, when boats were Bangkok's chariots.

An elephant has been causing trouble in the City again though on this occasion it seems to have been the fault of his driver. It was being driven along Rajani Road [paralleling Klong Lawd] and opposite the Ministry of Public Works it met a riksha. The driver of the elephant said the riksha puller abused him as he passed and he is alleged to have ordered his elephant to turn and attack the Chinaman. Anyhow, that is what the elephant did, squeezing the man with his trunk. Of course, the animal must have acted carefully and, one would think, without anger otherwise there would have been very little Chinaman left and apparently the man was not seriously injured.

—April 1900

We are glad to learn that in all probability the nuisance created by the manuring of market gardens in Bangkok will soon be done away with. The evil smell caused by the manure that most of these gardeners seem to prefer, often completely spoils some of the best drives in Bangkok and it is certainly injurious to the health of those who reside in the immediate neighborhood of these gardens...

...The loudest complaints in fact have come from foreigners whose drive out to Sapatoom has often been spoiled.

—July 1900

Note: Sapatoom Road is the former name for Rama I Road running between the Yodse Bridge and the Rajprasong intersection. It was also the name of an elite residential district.

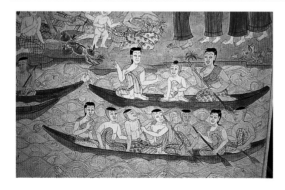

The motorcycle has penetrated to Bangkok.

—August 1900

independent sun — usually an enormous shopping mall covering several acres — with homes and small businesses arrayed around it. The city has ballooned westward. While in 1932 the Memorial Bridge plunged like a knife into untouched jungle, the steel and concrete of modern Bangkok blankets both riverbanks. Eight bridges now span the Chao Phya, with more under construction each year, stapling the twin halves of a city into a single entity. Since the 1970s, Thonburi — for 180 years regarded as a separate municipality — has been officially incorporated into Greater Bangkok. The old rice fields have sprouted thousands of shops and factories of every size, testament to the city's

A python 10 feet, four inches in length was found in the storeroom at the English Pharmacy this morning. It had got in during the night and, after upsetting a few bottles, had settled on a beam. A drug store, however, is not a place for a wise snake to frequent unless, of course, it is really anxious to have a new sensation. This one was offered chloroform and, when dazed by this new experience, it was pulled off its perch and had its account promptly settled.

—August 1900

When it was built in 1933, the Siam Society sat by itself in an empty field. Today, it is dwarfed by its neighbors.

increasing alienation from the farms that once sustained it. Bangkok's rural antecedents are reflected only in the design of shophouses — narrow fronts opening to the street and deep passages into the interior — which call to mind farms with a short frontage along a canal and a long narrow plot running back perpendicular to it.

These pages present a stereoscopic view of how the city's contours and its perspectives have metamorphosed over a single century. The choice of the years, 1900 to 2000, is arbitrary. In truth, we edge into the century when it is obvious that little remains from earlier eras or that now-familiar landmarks had not yet risen from the plains. For example, even 80 years ago what is now bustling Sukhumvit Road was only a country lane running between rice fields. A 1932 photo of the just-completed Siam Society headquarters on Soi Asoke (Soi 21) off Sukhumvit Road

shows a lone building standing forlorn in an empty field, suggesting it was one of the first structures to rise from the flat land. Aerial photographs taken in 1946 reveal a metropolis still seeking its edges, tentatively thrusting concrete fingers into the rice paddies. Such images provide visual anchors enabling us to comprehend the progression of the urban sprawl that would later characterize the city.

Left: A boy approaching puberty prepares for the tonsure ceremony wherein his topknot will be snipped off to symbolize his passage into adolescence.
Below: Modern conveniences rapidly found their way into Thailand and were welcomed by a public eager to own them in the early years of the century.

BANGKOK AT THE END
OF THE NINETEENTH CENTURY

A. Cecil Carter, Secretary-General of the Siamese Royal Commission to the Louisiana Purchase Exposition, and a long-time resident of Bangkok, in 1904 added these dimensions to the city's character:

"From the palace to the southeast stretches the New Road, the oldest of the roads built outside the city. Formerly an elephant track running parallel to the river, along the backs of the houses which faced the river, it now passes through a densely populated quarter and is the busiest road in the town. Lined on both sides by shops for some three miles, it is traversed by electric trams which follow one another every few minutes, while carriages, jinrikishas, bullock carts, and native omnibuses pass in perpetual stream.

"The river is hardly less crowded than the New Road. Both sides for miles above and below the palace are lined by floating houses, most of which are occupied by traders...Down the middle of the stream are anchored the ocean-going steamers flying the flags of many nations, sailing boats loading teak for the European and American markets, whilst in and out and from shore to shore scurry steam launches of every sort and shape. With the tide, huge rice-boats bring the harvest to the rice-mills, and rafts of teak logs, which may have been years on their journey from the north, follow a puffing launch which has picked them up above the city to tow them to the mill.

"Then there are house-boats, with two or more rowers; a priest's boat, paddled by ten of his pupils; boats which ply for hire and carry eight to twelve passengers, rowed and steered by one man like a gondola; tiny canoes, beyond the skill of Europeans to manage, holding just the postman and his bag of mail, or perhaps a travelling cook who, with his pot of boiling rice on a little stove in front of him and the rest of his cuisine cunningly stowed around him, drives a roaring trade with the boatmen and dwellers in floating houses, dispensing his goods with the one hand and keeping the boat steady with the other.

"The...foreign element [of the population] includes Chinese, Japanese, Koreans, Malays, Javanese, Hindus, Klings, Pathans, Afghans, Burmese, Arabs, Cambodians, Annamites, most of whom are rendered conspicuous by their national dress, which they seldom abandon."

— A. Cecil. Carter, *The Kingdom of Siam, 1904* [1]

Bangkok streets were more tranquil before the arrival of the automobile.

TWO CENTURIES
TWO CITIES

Period photographs encapsulate changes that words alone cannot convey. Thais were quick to take up photography, led by King Chulalongkorn (reigned 1868-1910), who encouraged his children to pursue the hobby. We have been bequeathed scores of photos by and of King Chulalongkorn and his family, many with his children clustered around an outsize view camera, peering intently into the lens.

Although many noble families were reluctant to peer through a viewfinder, they were quite eager to pose on the other side of the lens. The city boasted numerous photography studios; many of their proprietors recorded their impressions of the city in their spare time. Unfortunately, few photographers signed their works so that while today we have numerous superb

In 1908, King Chulalongkorn's 40th year as Thailand's monarch was marked by grand celebrations including the erection of an elephant gate on Rajdamnern Avenue. In 1996, the statue would be replicated at the head of Rajdamnern Klang Avenue for the 50th anniversary celebrations marking the accession to the throne of King Bhumibol Adulyadej in 1946.

pictures, we have no idea who took most of them. From advertisements we know that Robert Lenz, the preferred photographer of royalty, had a studio on Chalermkrung Road, as did J. Antonio, noted for his portraits of ordinary Thais. Francis Chitra was also popular and Nai Chayachitrakorn was famed for his soft style. Mr. Tekman in Yanawa was favored by Chinese clients who, in an age before color film, prized his color-tints.

The photographs left by early lensmen, juxtaposed with those taken in the present, reveal a city radically altered by time. In many instances, we are surprised by how much has survived from bygone days, whether entire buildings or only small motifs almost hidden among modern glass and concrete edifices.

Such photos piquantly illustrate changes in lifestyles and in altered perceptions of how a city should be used. For example, a

> A correspondent writes that King Chulalongkorn had a very pleasant time at Lop Buri and that being in so quiet a place he came into closer contact with the people of the district than he has perhaps ever done before with his ordinary subjects. He was very frequently out and about meeting with them and one day shortly before he left he had tiffin [afternoon tea] at the house of a Phu Yai Baan [village headman]. On the occasion of a religious festival held at the royal pavilion, His Majesty gave instructions that the people of the district should be permitted to join in the ceremonies. All this is very different from the old days when king and people hardly ever saw one another and no one can doubt that, even in Siam the change that His Majesty has made, is all for the better.
> —October 1900

King Chulalongkorn, fifth monarch of the Chakri dynasty, ruled Thailand from 1868 to 1910, initiating its transformation from a rural nation into a modern state. In 1900, he had been on the throne for 32 years and was 10 years away from being the longest-reigning monarch in Thai history. One hundred years later, King Bhumibol, ninth inheritor of the Chakri mantle, had been ruling for 54 years, surpassing his progenitor by one 12-year cycle.

century ago people used the streets as footpaths; there were no sidewalks. Many photographs depict citizens blithely ambling along a thoroughfare with an insouciance that would be suicidal in today's hurtling traffic. Only with the introduction of automobiles do we begin to see roads delineated into separate channels for vehicles and pedestrians.

It is also evident that the air used to be cleaner. Observe how clearly distant objects can be seen. It is probable that until the introduction of fossil fuels, smoke from wood and charcoal cooking fires was the only pollutant to haze the air. But natural fuels contributed such a small volume of particulate matter that their

A photography shop near Oriental Lane early in the 1920s when New Road was shared by cars, trams, rickshaws, and pedestrians.

blurring impact was far less noticeable than the exhaust fumes of the present day. One can also infer that with no cars, the old city was considerably quieter.

Early photographs also clearly show when electric and telephone wires began to score lines across the empty sky. The placement of wires is random — strung wherever they are needed — as if a brazen symbol of modernity, placed without any desire to keep them from defiling the passersby's field of vision. Could the early technocrats have imagined how their cables would proliferate? Today, virtual spaghetti tangles of wiring are the norm and it is the rare vista that is not marred by dozens of lines. Only on Silom Road have the cables been buried beneath the ground, denying the migrating barn swallows their winter perches. (Not that the birds have departed; curbside trees now bear their weight— and their annual whitewashing.)

Also conspicuously absent from the old photographs are the

In suits and bowlers, King Chulalongkorn's children pose with their father.

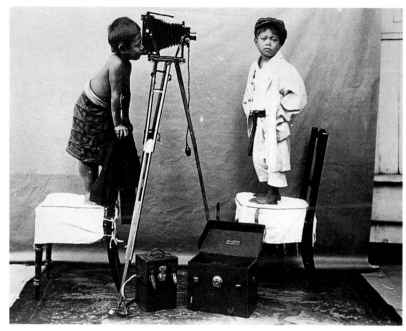

Whimsical shots resulted when photographers played in their studios.

high walls — many of them topped with glass shards or metal spikes — that separate many of today's houses and businesses from the street and from each other. In 1900, there were no iron bars on windows or metal grates on shop fronts. Buildings were set back from the street; many stores were fronted by wide lawns. The photographs suggest a friendlier age. Short picket fences or no fences at all, imply that residents communicated with passing strangers; that there existed a sense of community today found only in the villages.

There was a partial eclipse of the moon last evening rather less than a fourth of the moon's surface being covered by the earth's shadow. The Chinese and others in Bangkok beat gongs and fired crackers to scare off the dragon but it is doubtful if the belief in that dragon is very strong now.

—November 1901

The city was more open and less cluttered. *Wats* and government buildings were graciously set back from roads and canals, giving the passerby a vista and a sense of perspective. Only in Chinatown and the poorer districts were buildings clumped together, the Chinese having brought with them the narrow, snaking lanes and dense concentration of buildings typical of their native cities. As the century progressed, and as economic considerations rather than aesthetics came to dictate land use, intensive clustering would pervade

Looking west from the Golden Mount, one sees few differences over a century other than that most buildings have grown a story or two taller. The low roofs reflect an ancient law still in effect that buildings in the vicinity of royal palaces cannot be constructed higher than seven stories. To the right of center, the Grand Palace crowns the horizon; Wat Arun rises on the left. Near the center of the photograph is the Giant Swing and Wat Suthat.

the entire city. Open spaces would shrink, and then disappear, giving the city a sense of claustrophobia that earlier residents would have associated with Calcutta, Shanghai, and other teeming Asian cities.

The old photos show avenues lined by trees. By mid-century, city planners were quite casually chopping them down to widen streets. Even into the 1980s, trees were regarded as expendable impediments to the march of progress, as parasites whose roots disrupted

The latest Royal Gazette contains a proclamation which modifies the marriage laws of this country. In cases of divorce, the woman has hitherto been required to repay the money which the husband paid at the time of marriage. The new proclamation makes that unnecessary in the future.

—July 1900

We gave the other day a translation of a Siamese Mnemonic setting forth the correct colour of the *panung* [lower garment for men] for each day of the week. A correspondent writes that these are the correct colours and that the rule is observed in the Palace at least. He adds that no one except the King and the Princes may wear the red *panung* on Sunday; though on other days everyone may wear the proper colour of the day. The rule, however, does not seem to be generally observed now.

—February 1900

Before the invasion by the automobile, streets were for strolling, and were shared only with trams and rickshaws. This is Mahachai Road running along the inner face of the city wall.

21

communication cables and water lines, and whose boughs tangled the overhead electric wires. A welcome reversal of such destruction has occurred in the past decade. Streets bare of trees in the 1970s are now shaded by corridors of handsome foliage rising three stories into the air. Parks, though often only pocket-sized, are being created all over the city, in response to growing public clamor for a better quality of life. Many modern photographs show that — contrary to popular opinion — there are more trees today than there were a century ago.

Seekak Phyasi (formed by the intersection of New Road and Tanao Road) was at the heart of the business district. It held the tree-shaded Seekak Dispensary and numerous other handsome shops selling sundries, a quiet street frequented by few vehicles or pedestrians. Today, it's just another busy intersection on the route between Wat Phra Kaew and Chinatown.

Aerial photographs reveal that even as late as 1946, Bangkok remained a city of waterways. Look closely and you will see dozens of small feeder canals holding numerous medium-sized boats. In 1955, Klong Hualampong, the last of the major canals, was filled to widen Rama IV Road and most of the capillary channels were replaced by culverts. But even in the 1970s, canals still ran down one side of Henri Dunant Road and Soi Lang Suan; the two car lanes of Sathorn Road hemmed a tree-shaded canal. In the 1980s, many of the larger canals

Two passenger steam launches were yesterday on their way down to Bangkok from beyond Ayutthaya when a man on the river bank at Wat Po-Lien near Pathumthani shouted for one of them to pick him up. Both launches made for the river bank and the second crashed into the side of the first as the passenger was getting on board, doing considerable damage.

Then, there was a fight, of course, and revolvers were fired. But the passengers on both launches objected and the crews had to desist before any serious damage had been done. There are great possibilities for adventure on these river launches.

—May 1900

Above: Buildings have become billboards for advertising messages, often obscuring their beauty. Below: A survivor of the past just off New Road, steps from Seekak Phyasi, is festooned with electrical wires.

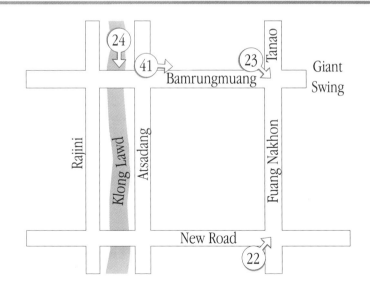

Below: The view south from the Chang Rongsee Bridge over Klong Lawd on Bamrungmuang Road. The area owes its name 'Rongsee' to the proximity of a sawmill that once operated nearby. The 'Chang' (Elephant) of its name, refers to the Saphan Chang or 'Elephant Bridges' that were built after the reign of King Rama I. By 1887, 15 of them spanned canals on key city roads. They  *were so named because they were sturdy enough to support the weight of elephants, either in war or peace time. The original bridge was modified in 1887, and again in 1910. Left: Decorating both ends of the Chang Rongsee Bridge are sculptures of dogs' heads, indicating the Chinese lunar year in which the span was re-built, 1910.*

still supported barge communities. At Bo Bae Market on Klong Padung Krung Kasem, produce was unloaded at the quayside, while in other canals dozens of barges served as permanent family homes. Today, only at the Chao Phya end of Klong Lawd, near the Memorial Bridge, are barges still moored. Sadly, even the riverine barge community at the foot of the Krung Thon Bridge is rapidly disappearing.

Perhaps the most unfortunate difference between then and now is the proliferation of signage. The old photographs show only a few signs and even those whisper their messages. Today, virtually every

building surface hosts huge signs that shout admonitions to buy, a garish museum for the advertising industry. Clearly, traditional Thai aesthetics have fallen victim to the clamor of mass consumption.

Similar clutter is found at ground level. Obstacle-course sidewalks sprout pipes, pylons, broken concrete, and the debris of long-forgotten projects. Canals are filled with squatter housing, of the detritus of abandoned civic projects. Scaffolding defaces renovation projects for months after the work is finished.

Evident also in the old photographs is the intimate association between the city and its river. The sharp division between land and water later provided by seawalls and buildings, is not yet apparent. Houseboats still linked the two elements, melding one into the other in a natural transition from land to liquid. In 1927, Erik Seidenfaden wrote, "alas the picturesque, floating houses have nearly all disappeared." [2] Only riverside hotels capitalize on Bangkok's historic association with its river, utilizing terraces and balconies to allow a full appreciation of its flowing beauty and balmy breezes.

> In the time of the old Regent, we understand, there was a regulation that no Siamese who held an official post could marry a European lady and retain his position under the Government.
> That was a harsh regulation but somehow it embodies the wisdom of an experience much wider than that of Siam. The objection to it is that it makes no provision for the exceptions to the rule and, so far as we know, Siam's little experience has gone to prove the rule chiefly by providing exceptions.
>
> —September 1900

Right: This barge community just below the Krung Thon Bridge is the last on Bangkok's rivers and canals. And in a few years, these barges, too, will be gone, victims of rising maintenance costs and moorage fees. Upper right: As in Bangkok's early days, Phak Klong Talat at the foot of the Memorial Bridge is a receiving dock for canal boats bringing produce from Thonburi gardens. From here, the vegetables will be distributed to city markets by truck.

BANGKOK'S GEOMETRY

Old photos show us how elements of Bangkok appeared but they reveal little of the city's overall structure or rationale. Then, as now, its principal feature was the Chao Phya River. The lower river was lined with wharves and warehouses, distribution points from which foreign goods fanned out through the city's markets. In the river's center were moored the ships of a dozen nations, shifting their cargoes to and from graceful wooden barges of a design still to be

found on the river today. Even in 1900, the foreshore was still lined five and six deep with floating houses covered by thatched roofs.

Most of Thailand's paved roads in 1900 were found within Bangkok's walls. Just in time, too, because by 1908 there were more than 300 cars crawling around the town.

Nonetheless, the pedestrian ruled and merchants regarded both the streets and sidewalks as display space. In *Twentieth Century Impressions of Siam* written in 1903, Arnold Wright and Oliver T. Breakspear noted a situation which still prevails in the city today: "The lower classes make use of the pavement as annexes to their houses and shops to such an extent that in many places the pavements have entirely disappeared. No law has yet been passed to prevent this overrunning the sidewalks, so that even when it is possible — as, for example, after a fire — to re-establish the alignment of the streets, there is difficulty in remedying the evil." [3]

Most of the population on the Bangkok bank was concentrated between Deves (Theves) — at the northern mouth of

Above: These clipper ships were a common sight on the Chao Phya River in an age when most boats were propelled by the wind or by strong-armed rowers. Below: Boats served as residences and vehicles for casual travel and goods transport, a way of life in old Bangkok that has all but disappeared.

Opposite page: The Chao Phya River today, looking downstream from the Phrapokklao Bridge, is still a transportation highway between the sea and the Central Plains.

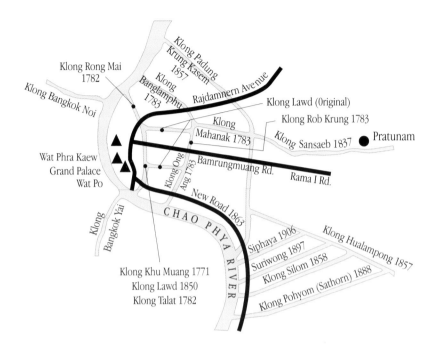

Klong Rong Mai 1782
Klong Padung Krung Kasem 1857
Klong Banglamphu 1783
Rajdamnern Avenue
Klong Bangkok Noi
Klong Lawd (Original)
Klong Rob Krung 1783
Klong Mahanak 1783
Klong Sansaeb 1837
Pratunam
Wat Phra Kaew
Grand Palace
Wat Po
Klong Ong 1783
Ang 1783
Bamrungmuang Rd.
Rama I Rd.
Klong Bangkok Yai
New Road 1863
CHAO PHYA RIVER
Siphaya 1906
Suriwong 1897
Klong Silom 1858
Klong Hualampong 1857
Klong Pohyom (Sathorn) 1888
Klong Khu Muang 1771
Klong Lawd 1850
Klong Talat 1782

Klong Padung Krung Kasem — and the southern extremity of New Road just past the present-day Bangkok Bridge, a band approximately 10 kilometers long. Bangkok's anchor was Ratanakosin Island, which held the Grand Palace, Wat Phra Kaew (Temple of the Emerald Buddha), and all of the city's principal royal and religious monuments. This 'island' was bounded on the west by the Chao Phya River and on the east by a canal dug in 1771 by King Taksin as a defensive moat. Called Klong Khu Muang Derm (Old City Canal) during the Ayutthaya and Thonburi periods, after 1782, the northern half was re-named Klong Rong Mai (Silk Factory Canal), and the southern half was called Klong Talat (Market Canal). By 1900, it was known by a third name, Klong Lawd ('Drinking Straw Canal' for its narrowness), although this name had originally applied to two smaller canals connecting Klong Lawd with Klong Rob Krung paralleling it to the east.

After 1783, Klong Lawd was encompassed by Klong Rob Krung (Canal Encircling the City), itself comprising two segments. The northern portion was known as Klong Banglamphu (Canal of the Village of the Lamphu or *Sonneratia* trees) which was demarcated by

It seems doubtful if even that useful personage, the oldest inhabitant, can remember so lengthy an extension of cool weather as we are having at present. Instead of a few mango showers in January and February, and otherwise unbroken drought and heat till into May, we have right along had the weather that one expects after the breaking of the monsoon. There certainly has not been anything like it for the past 15 years.

Is the climate changing and the terrors of the hot season becoming a thing of the past? Or shall we have to pay for the present pleasant weather by a long delay in the coming of the monsoon?
—March 1901

Built in the 1860s, the bridge from which this photo was taken was named for Prince Damrong, regarded as the father of Thai history, whose palace stood just to the west. The canal, Ong Ang, is now covered in tin shanties and the Golden Mount is obscured by tall buildings.

Phraumane Road. Its southern extension, Klong Ong Ang (*ong* is 'water jar', *ang* is 'bowl'; the principal goods sold there), was paralleled by Phrasumane Road's continuation, Mahachai Road. The latter canals had been dug by King Rama I (1782-1809), the city's first ruler, as a defensive moat and rimmed by a thick, crenellated brick wall (many of the bricks floated down on barges from ruined Ayutthaya) built by 5,000 Laotian prisoners of war. Excavation of a third canal, Padung Krung Kasem (i.e. 'maintaining urban happiness'; also called 'Klong Kut Mai' or 'Newly-dug Canal'), running from Deves to the present Royal Orchid Sheraton Hotel, was not completed until 1857.

On the advice of an important Buddhist monk, King Rama I had left the moats unbridged to deter invaders. By 1900, however, city waterways were crossed by more than 2,000 bridges, many of them

Above: This Klong Lawd drawbridge, modeled on a Dutch original, was typical of many built over city canals to allow the passage of boats. Called a 'Saphan Hok' (Lever Bridge) it was re-built for the Rattanakosin Bicentennial celebrations in 1982 marking 200 years as the nation's capital. Below: This 'Phra Roop' ('royal image' referring to its portrait of King Chulalongkorn) Bridge at Wat Benjamabophit was designed by Prince Naris and built in 1901.

very handsome structures. Most notable were the tall 'camel-hump' bridges, derived from Chinese design, which allowed the passage of large boats. The gradual lowering of bridge heights over succeeding decades — the spans seemingly compressed by the weight of increasing traffic — is emblematic of the decreasing importance of boats in moving goods and people within the city. Today, only a few 'camel-hump' bridges remain, the most notable example being found where Rama I Road crosses Klong Padung Krung Kasem and the railway tracks.

In 1890, the city wall encircling the old city was essentially intact. It was studded with 14 *pom* (watchtowers) spaced 400 meters

apart. Each *pom* was named for an event, a courageous animal, or a Hindu god. Some names were meant to strike fear into enemies. Pom Mahakan, named for Phra Kan, the Hindu God of Death, referred to the horrible fate bound to befall any enemy attempting to breach the gate. Pom Phrasumane was named for the mythical mountain which stands at the center of the universe. Pom Sua Tayarn, at the intersection of New Road and Mahachai Road, meant 'Leaping Tiger'. Until it was demolished in 1926, Pom Mahachai (Great Victory) dominated the intersection of Mahachai and Yaowaraj.

The city wall was also punctuated by tall gates. The best known was Pratu Phi (Spirit Gate) where Bamrungmuang Road

Until the end of the 19th century, Bangkok's streets belonged to animal-drawn conveyances but by 1908 cars were a common sight with more than 300 of them bumping noisily through the city. Here, passersby gawk as a cavalcade of cars, driven by princes and nobles and graced by their ladies, makes its way along Rajdamnern Road past Sanam Luang.

Everybody in Bangkok is presumably aware that there is superb road metal now to be seen (very plainly) on the roads. A brick road at its best is nothing very grand and is of short duration. But it is evident that the authority which tries to keep the roads in repair is now in a position to get a supply of capital road-making material. There is therefore no reason why we should not have splendid roads in Bangkok. If the authority in question — one always forgets which it is — could only catch someone who know how to make roads.

The present attempt to remake bits of New Road is a brilliant example of how not to do it. In the first place, there is a good deal of rainy season in Bangkok but curiously enough it is the dry season that has been selected to remake the principal thoroughfare.

Also, it is evident that the person responsible is not a Gymkhana Club 'owner' for these great patches of unrolled stones are enough to make any man give up all interest in his pony and trap. Cannot a roller be bought or borrowed somewhere?

It goes without saying that no one is responsible for the peculiar system of road mending now adopted. The Government has engineers in its service but the system seems to preclude responsibility falling on anyone. We shall only have improvement when such roadmaking is taken as a proof of incompetence on the part of some individual. Then, Bangkok ought to be able to boast of model roads.

—February 1901

penetrated the wall. Through it the dead were carried before cremation at Wat Saket, a temple which lies below the massive artificial mountain of Phu Khao Thong (the Golden Mount).

Within a few short years, the demands of progress dictated that watchtowers and gates be demolished to widen streets. In 1894, Pom Isinthorn Pan Fah was dismantled and the following year, the Pom Prachan was demolished. Today, of the five along the river and eight along Klong Rob, only two remain: Pom Mahakan (at Pan Fah on

Once bordered by the city wall, Phrasumane Road is now hemmed by buildings. All that remains is Pom Mahakan next to the Pan Fah Bridge where Rajdamnern Road exited the city through a tall gate on its way into the countryside towards the Dusit Palace and Vimarn Mek Palace.

Rajdamnern Road), and Pom Phrasumane (where Klong Banglamphu meets the river on Phra Athit Road).

From the royal hub of Ratanakosin Island, four spokes ran north, south, east, and northeast. Stretching to the north was Phra Athit Road, which was lined by palaces belonging to Thai princes, handsome buildings many of which now house international agencies and large companies. North of that is Samsen Road which also held

Looking north along Mahachai Road at its intersection with Yaowaraj Road, the Mahachai watchtower was demolished in 1926 and the offices of the B. Grimm Company were built on the site. The gates on the left led to Wang Burapha, Bangkok's largest and most magnificent palace.

many princely and noble homes.

The hub's second major spoke, Charoenkrung (New Road), ran southeast through the populous Chinatown, the seed of which had been planted in the 18th century. Prior to Bangkok's establishment, the Chinese merchant community had occupied an area north of Wat Po, and directly opposite Thonburi. When King Rama I sought to shift the throne for his new dynasty from Thonburi to Bangkok, he asked the

A couple of Indian dairymen were summoned to the British Counselor Court today for allowing their cattle to stray on the paddy fields at Sala Daeng [at the top of Silom Road where it converges with Rama IV Road]. Defendants were ordered to pay *Ticals* 20, the amount of the damage.

—December 1900

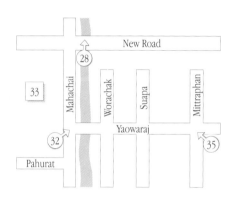

The original Wang Burapha Pirom — the palace at the center of the photo — was built in the reign of Rama I and expanded in the 1820s as a defensive fortress along the city's eastern wall. The magnificent palace in this 1946 photo was built between 1875 and 1881 but by the 1940s, it had fallen into disrepair. After the war, developers demolished the palace and erected shops and two cinemas, the Grand and King's. Here, looking southwest, Mahachai Road runs diagonally from the lower right corner to the Memorial Bridge, intersected at the palace gate by Yaowaraj Road running to the left.

merchants and their families to relocate to the southeast. This area, lying between the river and what later became New Road, grew into the city's Chinatown, a warren of lanes and tightly-bunched buildings replicating the cities of the Celestial Kingdom. On the land they vacated, King Rama I built the Grand Palace complex and Wat Phra Kaew, the Temple of the Emerald Buddha.

Sampeng Lane was Chinatown's principal thoroughfare until 1863 when it was joined by Charoenkrung (New Road), reputedly built and paved after the foreign community petitioned King Mongkut (Rama IV) for a proper street. For three decades, Sampeng and Charoenkrung were the only streets leading southeast from the royal city, but after a major fire destroyed a large portion of Sampeng in

> Yesterday afternoon an outbreak of fire was noticed in a house at Sam Yek. The door was locked but the police promptly burst it open and extinguished the fire before any great damage had been done. The door had been locked in the inside by an opium smoker who was still in the land of dreams when rescued by the police.
>
> —April 1900

Above left: As brutal as Thai boxing strikes some today, in 1900, it was even more violent. Boxers' hands were bandaged; unscrupulous promoters would embed ground glass in the wrappings to increase the damage. The boxer's only protection was a genital cup fashioned from half a coconut shell. Below left: In 1900, the government was just beginning to close the opium parlors, allowing the remaining addicts to dream out their lives but ensuring that new addicts would not be created. The marijuana that these three smokers inhaled was still tolerated; not until later in the century would it be outlawed.

Right: Tuuk Kow Chun (Nine-story Building) was a New Road pleasure palace offering an array of delights. The sybarite started on the ground floor with a gourmet meal, and ascended upwards — each floor offering an indulgence more provocative than the one before — until he arrived in 'heaven' on the top floor. The khanom jin (Chinese noodle) restaurant on the corner has been owned by the same family for more than 100 years.

1891, King Chulalongkorn authorized the construction of Yaowaraj as a third arterial through Chinatown.

By 1900, Sampeng Lane enjoyed a dual reputation as a center of commerce and the city's Sin Alley. Lined with gambling houses, it was regarded as Bangkok's Khom Khiew (Green Light) district, so named for the green lanterns that hung before the doors of its bawdy houses. Sampeng shared its tawdry reputation with Bumpen Boon Along (now buried beneath the Chalerm Krung Theater), which was known for its dingy pool halls and girly shows, 'Rung's Dancing Girls' being among the most popular.

The Chinese New Year is the fire season proper in Bangkok. On Tuesday evening, two important rice mills were burned down and there is naturally a strong suspicion that the fire owed its origin to the 'seasonable' firecracker. It is asserted, however, that the outbreak was due to an act of incendiarism, some persons having been seen throwing firebrands a little after eight o'clock...The damage is being put at Tcs. 500,000 but it will take more than that to replace the property destroyed. The insurance on one mill was renewed a couple of days before the fire, while the other had not yet been renewed.
—February 1900

Wright and Breakspear described this area by saying, "South of the walled city is the main commercial part of Bangkok. Along the riverside is a knotted congerie of narrow lanes, known as Sampeng, which in all their characteristics are an exact replica of a Chinese native city. Here are to be found the gaudily begilt opium dens, the theatres, maisons de plaisir, and similar institutions of Canton, with the addition of the gambling house. This district is the real 'bazaar' of Bangkok and in it almost any known article may be purchased" [4]

Today, many old Chinatown lanes have survived intact. The viewer is transported back 100 years as he walks past an ancient shrine, a small studio making Chinese lanterns, a spice shop selling meter-long slabs of cinnamon bark, and

Built after a disastrous fire ravaged Chinatown and fire brigades were unable to penetrate the narrow lanes with their water pumping wagons, Yaowaraj Road soon became one of the city's major thoroughfares. Here, horse carts, rickshaws, trams, and human labor were the principal modes of transportation.

yet another offering three-meter tall incense sticks.

   After exiting Chinatown, New Road jogged right and headed south, following the riverbank, running between rows of colonial-style buildings erected by European residents and mercantile firms. It ended 6.7 kilometers south of the palace at the river's edge, a place called Thanon Tok, literally, "the road drops (into the river)". Just before

Right: Even today, Chinatown holds numerous back alleys identical to those in a city in ancient China, and with inhabitants from the Middle Kingdom as well. Far right: Monks look down on New Road from an upper story of Wat Leng Nuai Yee (Wat Mangkorn, or 'Dragon Wat'), one of Chinatown's principal Mahayana Buddhist sanctuaries.

Sathorn Road in 1946 still ran through a residential area interspersed with vegetable gardens. Those empty areas that would later be filled with tall buildings that would obscrure the landmark Christ Church on Convent Road, on the upper right of the earlier photograph.

reaching its terminus, New Road passed through Bangkolem, one of the city's elite foreign neighborhoods, a role that by the 1960s would be assumed by Phaholyothin and Sukhumvit Roads. "To the south and east of Sampeng is Bangrak, where most of the foreign legations and the majority of the banks and offices of Western business people are situated, and from thence to Bangkolem Point there is a long string of rice and saw mills, docks, ironworks, etc." [5]

New Road sprouted its own spokes, all running eastwards into districts with few houses and many produce gardens. Construction of the first of these canal/streets (the earth excavated from the canal was used to raise the roadbed above the annual floods), Silom 'Windmill'

Road (so-called for the devices that drew water from its canal to irrigate the adjacent fields) was financed by the government and completed in 1858. The three roads that soon paralleled Silom, however, were private initiatives by the city's first land developers. After excavating a canal and building the road, the developers were permitted to sell the land on either side to private buyers.

The first of these thoroughfares paralleling Silom was Sathorn (named for the noble who financed it), excavated in 1888. Suriwongse Road, completed in 1897, was the work of Chao Phya Suriwongse-wattanasak). The third, built without a canal, was called Siphya Road (*Si* means 'four', *Phya* — a non-hereditary title that until 1932 was bestowed on government officials of the second-highest rank — means

Right: This metal sculpture erected in 1998 at the intersection of Narathiwatrangsarit Road and Silom Road, is a reminder of the windmills (silom) *that once drew water from Klong Silom to irrigate vegetable gardens that stretched either side of it and lent their name to the road and canal. Such windmills — made of bamboo and fabric — can still be seen drawing sea water into the salt flats along the edge of the Gulf of Thailand in the region around Samut Sakhon southeast of Bangkok.*

Right: Klong Sathorn was originally called 'Klong Pohyom' ('Father Yom Canal') after the man who excavated it and sold the adjoining land to homeowners. The title later given to Poh Yom by King Chulalongkorn contained a new element, 'Sathorn', by which the canal later came to be known. There is little hint in this early photo of the concrete strip and concealed canal that characterizes Sathorn Road today.

Center: These two views of Bamrungmuang Road leading east towards the Golden Mount, Pratu Phii, and Wat Suthat are, at first glance, virtually identical. In the earlier photograph, however, the Giant Swing is 30 meters to the left of the road while in the present, it sits dead center. Modern residents could not recall that the poles had been moved. The mystery was solved with the discovery of a news item in a March 1900 issue of the Bangkok Times newspaper which read, "We understand that the big swinging poles [Giant Swing] opposite Wat Suthat at the platform on which they stand, are to be removed to the middle of the road [which will] be very much widened [with] a carriageway on either side of the platform." The resulting space became the city's largest fresh market, Talat Sao Ching Cha.

Below, far right: The Giant Swing ceremony was discontinued in the latter years of King Rama VII's reign (1925-1935) but in its heyday it was an annual event. According to Brahmin belief, Phra Isuan descended from heaven to earth for 10 days each year and during his stay, had to be entertained. Four men seated cross-legged on the swing seat, set it moving, climbing higher and higher towards a bamboo pole holding a small bag containing three tamlung, equal to 12 baht. When the swingers' arc approached 180 degrees, one man would lean outward to snatch the bag. Miscalculations could result in injury and even death. If they were successful, the next team would vie for a prize of 10 baht; the third team, for eight baht. The present swing poles were erected in 1919 by the Louis T. Leonowens company to honor their founder, the son of Anna Leonowens (of 'King and I' fame), and a successful businessman.

'Lord'. In fact, there were five developers including a *Luang* later elevated to the rank of *Phya*; had he been *Phya* at the time of construction, we would know the road as Haphya, *ha* meaning 'five'). This three-year project was completed in 1906. The segment of New Road between Sathorn and Siphya roads boasted three banks, a French hospital (St. Louis), a British nursing home on Convent Road, and the offices of English, French, Danish, German, and American doctors, besides numerous Siamese hospitals and medical men.

A third major spoke began at Wat Phra Kaew and ran due east along Bamrungmuang Road past the Giant Swing, and through Pratu Phii. As the city grew, Bamrungmuang Road was extended a number of times, each addition meriting its own name. The portion from Padung Krung Kasem Canal to the Rajprasong intersection with Rajdamri Road was named Rama I Road. The section from Rajprasong east to the railway tracks became Ploenchit. When it was extended once again, the new portion was named Sukhumvit Road.

RAJDAMNERN AVENUE IN THE YEAR 1900

In 1980, Nai Kanchanakkhaphan reminisced about the Rajdamnern Avenue he had known 80 years before.

There were two elephant stalls beside the City Shrine (Lak Muang, which was set in a park). The park was where in winter the circuses were held. 'Hippodrome' and 'Harmston' were two of the famous circuses that put up their big tents each year.

The first section of Rajdamnern Avenue [from Wat Phra Kaew to Phanphipopleela Bridge] was an undivided road, surfaced with gravel and deeply potholed. From Phanphipopleela Bridge, one could look down the avenue of tamarinds and see the oval curve of the low white rail fencing [around Sanam Luang]. Beyond the curve in the fence was the Pom Phadet Datsakon angle tower [at the northeast corner of Wat Phra Kaew] with its tall flagmast and the Siamese flag fluttering on high which stood at the corner of the white-washed, crenellated Grand Palace walls.

Rajdamnern Klang [from Phanphipopleela Bridge to Pan Fah] had parallel traffic dividers. Street lamps were gas powered and lit on moonless nights only; the same through the city. At 8 p.m., all lamps all over town were turned off for a moment, all at the same time. People set their clocks by it. The Avenue was clean, outstandingly

An oxcart trundles along Rajdamnern Avenue towards the Phanphipopleela Bridge, built in 1904 across Klong Lawd. 'Phanpipop' means Lord of Life. 'Leela' means movement i.e. where the King passed on his various duties. Early Rajdamnern was divided into three lanes; vehicles used the outer two lanes and pedestrians walked the inner one. The lanes were separated by islands dotted with park benches and mahogany trees that allowed one to walk the entire length of the road in shade.

beautiful, empty of people and traffic. I remember once sitting in a gig coming out of Si Yaek Khok Wua [Cow Pen Intersection, now called Tanao intersection] and turning down Rajdamnern Klang, I turned and looked both ways but saw no one on the street in any of the three blocks.

Si Yaek Khok Wua was where an Indian and his wife once kept cattle. The northern side of Rajdamnern Klang adjoined open

ground. There were two or three houses that traded in wood shavings used as insulation for ice. They used the open ground to dry the wood shavings. On the other side of the road there were two or three lanes leading to a residential area. Near the second intersection, but off the main road was [and is] the Satrividya Secondary [Girls'] School, known for its beautiful teachers and pretty schoolgirls.

There were two or three park benches on the road in front of the girls' school, but when school broke out the girls would all go home and the place was left deserted until the evening when the place became a well-known romantic spot.

At Pom Mahakan and the city wall down Mahachai, there was a narrow rectangular gap in the wall called the Pratu Chong Kut gate. When I was young I went through this gate many times to watch the *likay* performances arranged by the then famous Phraya Phet — along the *klong* in the other direction were timber yards [there still are].

The neighborhood between the Pan Fah Bridge and the Saphan Mahathai Uthit was called Sanam Khwai, [Water Buffalo Pen]. It was the part of town where *likay* and *lakhon chatri* theatrical groups lived [one still exists just down Larn Luang Road from Pan Fah], and in some cases performed. The house of a theatrical group would have a distinctive decoration out in front. Swords, staffs, knives, etc. were put in a cone on top of a short post together with a small red flag. This signified that the house belonged to a *lakhon chatri* group and was currently available for hire.

— Kanchanakkhaphan, "I Knew the Area 80 Years Ago" [6]

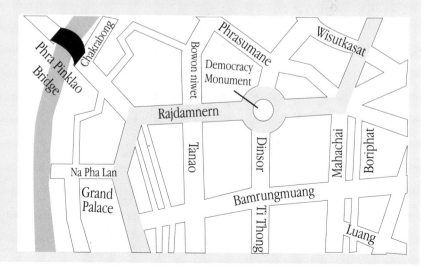

A fourth spoke from the Ratanakosin Island hub was still under construction in 1900. Called Rajdamnern (Royal Walk) Avenue, it ran northeast towards Vimarn Mek (Paradise Palace) in Dusit Park which King Chulalongkorn would complete that year as a rural residence and a more relaxed alternative to the formal Grand Palace. The same year also saw the completion of the city's last major Buddhist temple, Wat Benjamabophit, known to foreigners as the Marble Temple for the Carrera marble cladding it.

From the juncture of New Road and Klong Padung Krung Kasem, another key road branched to the east. Called Thanon Trong (Straight Street), it ran along the 5.18-km. Hualampong Canal, excavated in 1857 at the request of European traders who wanted a shorter route from their warehouses in Phrakanong to the city center. This canal eliminated a 20-km. journey along the river's tortuous bends to reach the wharves along Songwat Road. In 1900 the canal — later renamed Rama IV Road — was bordered by a roadway shared by cars,

Three steel arch bridges were built across major city canals in the third quarter of the 19th century. This one, Noraratana Sathan Bridge — sited where Chakraphong Road (running from Rajdamnern Avenue to Chakraphong's northern extension, Samsen Road) crosses Klong Banglamphu just north of Khaosarn Road — was replaced by a concrete bridge early in the twentieth century.

trams, and a small railway that plied a route southeast to Paknam.

Similarly, Larn Luang (Royal Nephew) — running east from Rajdamnern Klang (Middle Royal Walk) at Pan Fah — became Thanon Phra Cha Chin (named for a mythical Chinese road, and later called Petchburi Road) once it crossed the railway tracks. Until 1960, Petchburi terminated at entrance to the Pratunam (Watergate) Market. Built in 1908, the market was a quiet commuters' hub where people traveling by the mailboats to and from Phrakanong via Sansaeb Canal (dug in 1837 as an extension of Klong Mahanak) transferred to carriages for the ride into the city.

Right: Prince Naris, King Chulalongkorn's half-brother, was considered one of the most accomplished artists of his day. In 1899, he designed Wat Benjamabophit, the Marble Wat, which was completed in 1901.
Below left: Prince Naris' masterpiece, Wat Benjamabophit is a riot of detail rendered in gold leaf and tiny mirrors. The interior is illuminated by sunlight streaming through stained glass windows.

STREET LIFE

From contemporary descriptions, one can visualize a typical street on market day. Shopfronts extend goods-laden shelves into the road — there are no sidewalks — blurring the division between the buildings and the street. Store awnings shade shoppers wearing turbans, caps, topis, and other headgear, and clothed in caftans, sarongs, dhotis, and the garb of a dozen nations. Barefooted or sandaled, they gingerly step across open drainage ditches to reach the stalls. At one corner, carts await passengers, the horses switching their tails across their rumps to chase away pestering flies. At another corner, cone-capped coolies sit on the drawbars of their rickshaws rolling rough tobacco in banana-leaf wrappers, and gossip in low voices while scrutinizing passersby for potential customers.

A fine carriage struggles to make headway, obstructed by pedestrians who rule the roads, crossing wherever they wish. The

Aside from the tall buildings looming over the shophouses and the addition of sidewalks, little has changed on New Road between Silom and Sathorn roads.

46

carriage adds to the swirling dust kicked up cows being driven to the Thanon Tok abattoirs. Vendors shout their wares: sweets, betelnut, or nostrums, homemade perfumes, and sundries from around the world. Mangy dogs scavenge for scraps in the fly-blown garbage heaps.

Jostling for space, hand-drawn carts transport produce from the docks to the markets. Creaking wheels screech above the babble of Thai mangled by a dozen different tongues. From a back alley comes the clang of iron striking iron as a blacksmith beats metal into horseshoes or a carter repairs the leaf spring of a carriage. In another lane, muted hammering reveals a cooper crafting crates and barrels used in an age before cardboard boxes. Clacking looms turn out cloth, while a humming treadle-powered lathe shapes a leg for a teak table.

Despite the noise of milling people, the street is quiet when compared to the machine-generated clamor of today's thoroughfares. Only occasionally does a furiously-rung tram bell break the hum of commerce. A Sikh policeman with his imperious turban blows his whistle ceaselessly in a vain effort to bring order to the streets. The air reeks with the stench of raw sewage, of the cloying scent of incense from a Chinese shrine, and the searing odor of chilies sizzling on a *wok*. An elegant lady on her way home, clasps a lavender-soaked handkerchief to her nose as she steps daintily over the ditch.

And overhead, the sun beats down with hammer-like ferocity.

The other evening a prominent Siamese Minister had his hat snatched off his head in Worachak Road.

—August 1900

Note: M.R. Butri Viravaidya recalls hearing her elders talk of hat snatching. The valuable hats were made of woven peacock feathers. From an upper window, the snatcher would often tie a gecko to a string and lower it onto the hat of an unsuspecting wearer. When the gecko sank its claws into the hat the snatcher would reel up his prize.

Right and Below: Little has changed in the work methods followed in Bangkok's markets in the past century. Women still sell dried salted fish and commodities brought daily from farms on the outskirts of the city. The task of moving goods from boats to the city's markets still requires back-breaking labor, as seen here in the city's principal fresh market, Phak Klong Talat at the Bangkok end of Saphan Phuut, the Memorial Bridge.

THE IMPRINT
OF ITS INHABITANTS

Who were the people who lived in Bangkok in 1900? The population appears to have been amazingly diverse, with scores of ethnic groups: Chinese, Malay, Tamil, Bengali, Pathani, Burmese, Ceylonese, Khmer, Lao, Javanese, Shan, Mon, Vietnamese, and a dozen tribes. Photographs show streets filled with costumes representing nearly every Asian culture and much of the rest of the world.

The vast majority of the populace was Thai, although that term is almost impossible to define. The original Thais seem to have been an amalgam of indigenous peoples, Siamese, Lao, Mon, and other Asiatics. Since ancient times, the Thai strain had been augmented by a sizable influx of Indians and Chinese who had played pivotal roles in Siam's mercantile life, an infusion that accelerated in 16th century Ayutthaya. Added to the mix were Japanese in the hire of the royal court, Persian merchants, Arabic mercenaries brought by the French, and diverse travelers who had fallen in love with Thailand, married

According to our Chiang Mai correspondent, the law recently enacted for the purpose of doing away with slavery in Chiang Mai is, at least temporarily, working hardship among the 'Lao Poong Dam'.

The law is posted on the public highways and on the Courthouse doors but in effect, he asserts, things are not altogether what they seem. There are different classes of slaves and it seems a master may successfully transfer his men from one class to another. He then continues:

"There are good points in almost all of the new departures the Siamese have instituted up here. It is probably a good idea to prevent the sudden letting loose of all these slaves on a particular day with a flourish of trumpets. England said 'five years' to the people of Chieng Tung [in northern Burma] and then went to work to provide something to take the place of the 'paternal' system of the Chaos [princes]. Most of the household slaves are a bad lot in consequence of their environment; and they will need looking after till they learn to settle down to an honest home life.

"There is a large populace of so-called serfs up here, self-respecting men and women with homes of their own. They are continually at the mercy of their masters. The present laws ought to see that this class is freed at once. There ought to be no haggling over this business."

—August 1900

Note: Abolished in 1895 in Bangkok and some parts of Siam, slavery was banned nationwide in 1905.

A price and four retainers garbed in ceremonial northern war costumes pose before the gate to his house some time after the turn of the twentieth century. At this point, slavery had been abolished throughout the kingdom but many former serfs elected to work for their one-time masters.

local women, and set up housekeeping. Through the farsightedness of King Chulalongkorn, the institutions of slavery and serfdom had been abolished so the newcomers, like the Thais, worked and lived as free men. Europeans had been welcome in Ayutthaya until the events of 1688, when most were expelled, only to be welcomed back after 1830.

The spirit of tolerance and assimilation is evident in the creation of a new city to replace Ayutthaya, destroyed by the Burmese

Right: Chao Chom Choe Bunnag, one of King Chulalongkorn's wives, is representative of the prominence that foreigners of all nations had attained in Thailand's tolerant atmosphere. Her family, the Bunnags, had arrived from Persia to serve the kings of Ayutthaya as financial advisors. Her attire is also emblematic of the heights attained by upper class woman after Chulalongkorn encouraged them to participate in public life. His consort, Queen Saowapha, served as the kingdom's regent when the King traveled to Europe on a state visit. Below: An elegant elderly woman at her toilet late in the last century displays the cropped hair and clothes worn by women until King Chulalongkorn began modernizing his kingdom.

49

in 1767. Almost from its inauguration as the capital in 1782, Bangkok was welcoming outsiders. Some came as war prisoners pressed into service to build the new city's defensive walls and moats. On completing their work, they were allowed to remain, to began new lives as Thai citizens. Political refugees from neighboring nations were also given sanctuary and soon established their own neighborhoods.

Left: Chinese emigre Wang Lee went from rice milling to banking as the century progressed; the family mansion still stands on the Thonburi riverbank. Below: Built in 1915, the Chinese Chamber of Commerce on Sathorn Road was a meeting place for the city's richest merchants. Today, the abandoned hall is dwarfed by the Thai CC Tower, the chamber's new home.

Add to this cultural cauldron the traders from every realm who had since the 16th century been drawn to Siam's shores by its wealth of products and its free trade policies, and the picture which emerges is of a vigorous, progressive, polyglot metropolis.

Of their exact numbers, there are no official records, but contemporary observers estimated that the city held between 500,000 and 600,000 residents, including some 1,000 Europeans and North Americans. Poll tax registrations revealed the presence of 65,345 Chinese-born males; extrapolating from that figure, commentators estimated a further 20,000 elderly men, women, and children who paid no taxes, and arrived at a probable total Chinese population of around 85,000. The low number of women suggests that most of the Chinese were single men drawn to Thailand by the promise of employment. Working for low wages, they were financially incapable of bringing wives from China, so either remained single — hoping to return to China to marry — or married local women.

But while the sons of the Celestial Empire were undoubtedly the largest segment of the non-Thai population, they were only one component of a rich ethnic mix. Many Bangkok neighborhoods reflected the national origins of their inhabitants. Within the city wall lay Ban Tanao, comprising Mons who had migrated from Tenasserim in Burma. The road running through their community, Thanon Tanao, became known as the street of perfume makers, first for the women of the royal court, and later for the general public.

In "Ti Thong" (Beat Gold) Street, craftsmen still place gold nuggets between deer skins and hammer them to the thinness of gold leaf; one pound of gold can be flattened to cover a football field. Below: In Ban Baht (Village of Alms Bowl Makers) near Wat Saket, craftsmen use ancient technology to fashion the bowls carried by Buddhist monks on their morning bintabaht (alms rounds). The artisans have been challenged by more efficient machinery; today, Ban Baht is on its last legs.

On the corner of Rajdamnern and Phrasumane roads, the Thai Niyom Building was built atop the former palace of a Khmer noble. On upper Samsen Road was Ban Yuan (Village of Vietnamese) and just south of it was Ban Kamain (Village of Cambodians). Ban Tawai in Yanawa had been named for Mon timber merchants who hailed from Tavoy, Burma. Ban Kaek was home to Muslims; while off Rajaparob Road, Makassan was inhabited by refugees from the seaport of Makassar in Indonesia. Near Issaraphap Road in Thonburi was Ban Lao, named for its Laotian inhabitants. That many of these enclaves bore the name Ban or 'village' suggests rural associations. It is highly probable that in the early days when city walls faced jungle and rice fields, these were actual villages that were ultimately engulfed by the growing city.

A parade marches south down Ti Thong Road at the turn of the century. The roof of Wat Suthat is visible above the shops on the right.

The city still maintained vestiges of its earlier incarnation as a conglomeration of craftsmen's villages many of which left their names on streets and neighborhoods. These include Ban Moh (Potters' Village), Dinsor Road (originally, 'Dinsor Village' inhabited by makers of a chalk-like writing implement), Ti Thong Road (originally, 'Ban Ti Thong' or 'Village of Gold Beaters' named for artisans who pounded gold into gold leaf to be applied to Buddha images and other holy objects), Ban Baht (Village of Alms Bowl Makers), Ban Bu (burnishers of the prized brass bowls in which one served water to special guests or washed one's face each morning), Ban Dok Mai Fai (makers of fireworks), Ban Chang Lor (casters of metal objects including Buddha images), and Ban Kamin (Turmeric Powder Blenders). Others village

and community names reflected geographical features or commemorated famous battlefields of the Ayutthaya period: Lard Prao (Coconut Slope), Din Daeng (Red Earth), Phran Nok (Bird Hunter), Suapa (Wild Tiger), Kluai Nam Thai (Thai Banana).

Ban Moh began life as a Potter's Village but soon evolved into a goldsmith's street. From 1880 to 1940, its shops offered luxury items to upscale buyers. Although many gold shops remain on Pahurat Road, the intersection is now occupied by appliance dealers. Right: A reminder of Ban Moh's former incarnation has been sculpted on a shophouse wall.

MUNICIPAL SERVICES

The first quarter of the 19th century had witnessed a somewhat insular people pre-occupied with re-building their shattered kingdom after Ayutthaya's destruction by the Burmese. Xenophobia, a natural consequence of misuse by invading neighbors and grasping foreigners alike, was only gradually giving way to a benevolence towards outsiders. In the 1680s, a Greek adventurer, Constans Phaulkon, had risen rapidly to become Phra Klang (Treasury Minister,

the equivalent of Prime Minister), and he used his position to favor the French in their campaign to establish their dominance and proselytize the Catholic faith. Phaulkon might well have succeeded had not his patron, King Narai, died in 1688. The King's successors lost no time in expelling most foreigners, slamming shut the kingdom's doors until the 1830s when they were tentatively opened to Western merchants.

King Mongkut (reigned 1851-1868) and his son, Chulalongkorn, sought to strengthen their kingdom by inviting foreign advisors to work in key government ministries, imparting their knowledge of modern administrative methods to Thai officials. King Chulalongkorn also sent many of his sons to study new technology in

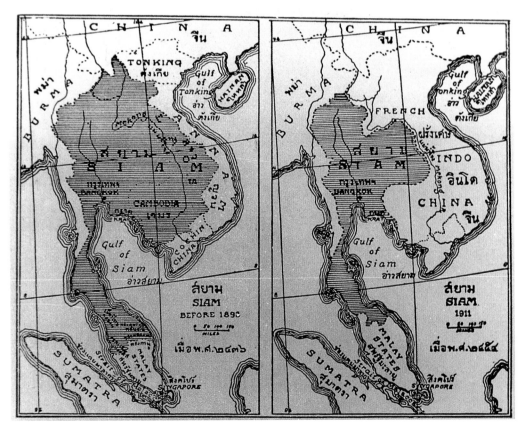

Left: Thai concerns about foreign domination were not misplaced. A series of nine land concessions between 1893 and 1911 nibbled away bits of the kingdom so that at his death, King Chulalongkorn ruled a realm half as large as the one he had inherited from his father, King Mongkut. Thus, the adoption of foreign technology was, in part, a means of defence in preserving what remained of a shrinking kingdom.

Right: Looking south along Mahachai Road towards the Damrongsathit Intersection at New Road, the inspiration for the design of the buildings is clear. This photo was taken about 1910 from a bridge over Klong Wat Suthat running next to Bangkok's Central Prison. The canal remains but the bridge has been replaced by culverts. Above right: The Damrongsathit Intersection was dominated by the very European-style Thai Niyom Department Store which later moved to the Thai Niyom Building at Pan Fah. The kiosk in the intersection was intended to raise a traffic policeman above the road and protect him. The kiosks were later removed because so many were toppled by speeding vehicles. Pratu Sam Yod, at the head of New Road, was one of the most important gates in the wall that ringed the old city.

European capitals and on their return, appointed them to administrative posts. Both foreign merchants and returning princes introduced new inventions and products to a society eager to adopt any technology which would improve their lives and keep the European colonizers at bay. To their credit, the Thais were confident enough in the resilience of their culture not to fear that they might be undone by

modernity. That self-confidence made them unlike many neighboring monarchies which rejected Western innovations outright, fearing that the foreigners and their inventions would usurp their power and corrupt their culture.

For most of the 19th century, Bangkok had been compact enough that canal boats and ox carts were sufficient to move its citizens about. But nearing the end of the century, Bangkok had grown large enough to necessitate a more comprehensive, land-based transportation network. The first step towards modern mass transit began on September 22, 1888, when a four-horse team tugged an iron tram along shiny tracks laid the length of New Road. Soon, horse-teams were pulling loads of passengers down major arterials within the walled city. Additional horses stationed along the routes helped their colleagues haul overloaded trams over the high bridges. In 1889 the trams were pressed into service in Chinatown when violence broke out between rival gangs. Trams rushed police into the heat of a five-hour battle that left 30 gangsters dead, hundreds wounded, and 800 in jail.

On April 11th, 1893, the horse trams were joined by the nation's first steam railway, a 22.5-kilometer line that ran between Bangkok's Hualampong Station and Paknam, along the future Rama IV Road, and then southeast to Samut Prakarn (Paknam). Although designed as a strategic link to speed troops quickly to protect

Above: The Electrical Store at Wat Lieb (also known as Wat Rajburana) sold appliances run by the city's wondrous new source of power. The Wat Lieb electricity generating plant was destroyed by Allied bombs in World War II, but this building, now designated a historical monument, was spared. Left: The latest imported goods could be found in a dozen department stores.

Bangkok's riverine gateway from seaborne invasion, it soon evolved into a passenger route. The train also enabled foreign residents to flee the sweltering city and to take the salt air along the Gulf of Thailand, in essence creating the country's first beach resort.

In the same year, the tram horses were retired. The newly-inaugurated oil-fired electricity generating plant at Wat Lieb (known formally as Wat Rajburana), near the future Memorial Bridge, enabled Bangkok to become the first Asian city to have electrified trams (Japan, and Copenhagen, would not switch to electric trams until 1903). The Wat Lieb plant, operated by the Siam Electricity Company, made Bangkok a pioneer in urban electrification. Houses and streets were now lit by electricity, a brighter, safer, and cheaper alternative to gas lights. The August 29, 1891 edition of the *Bangkok Times* reported that The Oriental Hotel "has electric lights in every room as of Wednesday last." The city was also a pioneer in the use of telephones. Late in 1891, the paper noted that "The Bangkok Hotel (on New Road) telephone number is 48." In every respect, Bangkok was shedding its rustic roots to become a modern city, equal to any in Asia.

Unfortunately, the rush to develop ignored a need for some basic utilities. With no public water system, private wells provided drinking water. Ordinary Thais imbibed rainwater or, during the hot season when no rain fell, drank from the river and canals — the very

Symbol of new prosperity: Wires ensnaring a house.

After reading the instructions issued to Paris policemen for treatment of persons struck by falling electric wires, a good many people will object to being resuscitated and will prefer death.

The process is to lay you on your back, and pull your tongue vigorously in and out of your mouth at a rate of twenty times a minute for an hour.

This is the penalty we pay for the telegraph, the telephone and the electric tram. Let us go back to the dear old days of the two-penny paper and the stage coach. It was a much happier world then, and nobody seized your tongue and pulled it out twenty times a minute in the name of humanity.

—August 1901

Note: Bangkok was one of the first cities in Southeast Asia to have electricity. By 1897, the entire city was electrified but not everyone was pleased, as evidenced by this piece.

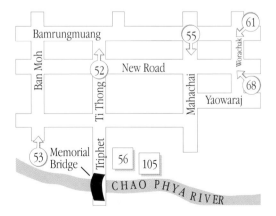

TRAMS, A WAY OF LIFE

For 70 years the tram was the city's principal mode of public transportation. Everybody rode them: army officers, businessmen, senior government officials, foreigners, tourists, princes, ladies, even children on their way to expensive private schools (imagine!).

Trams were not the most comfortable of conveyances. The windows had no glass, only tarpaulin shades which could be rolled down to block out the rain or sun. The drivers were also unprotected; during the monsoon season they were issued raincoats.

The cars were starkly utilitarian, their exteriors painted a drab khaki. A sturdy cowcatcher cleared the tracks of obstructions,

particularly stray buffaloes on their way to the slaughterhouses at the end of New Road. On reaching the terminus, the driver would unbolt the heavy iron 'plow' and move it to the other end of the car for the return journey.

Most cowcatcher victims were mangy street dogs, jaywalkers, the deaf, drunks, inattentive pedestrians, or the opium-hazed. In the 1890s a Danish driver inadvertently bagged a tiger that had been prowling near the slaughterhouses.

Tram drivers were the daredevils of the streets. Like the trams they drove, they were clad in khaki, wearing shorts or trousers with a black stripe running down the leg to distinguish them from conductors. Although the early trams had been driven by foreigners, mostly Danes, by 1900 Thais had taken over the well-paying jobs.

Drivers were subject to strict spot inspections and were heavily fined or dismissed for carelessness; even yawning on the job could reduce their pay packet. Unfortunately, such strictures did little to curb their exuberance especially their habit of careening around corners, a practice that amused some passengers, and horrified others. Turnouts were sited every 200 meters so as to allow two trams to pass each other, but macho operators played a game of chicken, charging the turnouts at full tilt, with bells madly clanging. Usually the trams slipped past each other with centimeters to spare, but if the driver misjudged, one or even both would be knocked off the tracks. Trams also frequently clipped passing cars or horse carriages.

Although originally intended only to warn pedestrians, the trams' footbells soon evolved into a sophisticated medium for

Dignitaries and drivers in spiffy uniforms celebrate the inauguration of tram service in 1893. The trams would move people from one end of the city to the other for 75 years before being retired from service. As had pedal rickshaws in the 1950s before they would be deemed too slow for fast city streets and thus impediments to speedier traffic.

communication. Drivers challenged or conversed with the bells, often arranging bets on races or boxing matches, their feet furiously pumping out tips and odds without a single spoken word. A driver could lose his entire pay packet on a few clangs of his bell.

There were strict rules for riders. Men had to wear at least a shirt and a *pakoma* to be allowed to ride even second class coaches. Durians had to be wrapped securely to mask their odor. No luggage was allowed although special dispensation was given to betel-chewing ladies, who were allowed to carry their betelnut baskets. During World War II, ladies were required to wear hats in first class but could ride bare-headed in second class. A convivial atmosphere pervaded the coaches and it was not unusual for a romance to blossom during the course of a ride.

There were four key lines. The longest (nine kilometers) and most popular, the Bangkolem line, began at the northeast corner of Wat Phra Kaew, ran south along its wall, then turned east to follow New Road to reach the end of the line at Thanon Tok. The first-class fare from Wat Phra Kaew to Bangkolem was 24 *att* (64 *att* = 1 *tical* as the *baht* was then called; in 1904 one pound sterling bought 16.67 *tical*. Thus the fare was 38 cents; the second-class fare was 12 *att*). About 25,000 passengers rode the tram each day, so many that the authorities soon hooked on a second car to handle the demand.

The Samsen line began in the north at Bangkrabu, ran south along Samsen Road and through the city, crossing the Bangkolem line at Samyaek in Chinatown and ending at the Paknam Railway Station on Rama IV Road. The 500-meter long Asadang line and 800-meter long Rachawong lines connected the main line with Phak Klong Talat (at the foot of the Memorial Bridge) and Rachawong ferry landings, respectively. Another line circled the inside of the old city wall. By the 1930s feeder lines ran from Silom to Pratunam, from Yodsae Bridge on Rama I Road to Pratunam, and from Wat Lieb near the Memorial Bridge to Nang Lern. Trams ran at four-minute intervals throughout the day and less frequently at night.

The earliest tram route, the Bangkolem line, started at Lak Muang (the city pillar) and ran along the eastern wall of the Wat Phra Kaew complex before turning east along New Road. Stops were denoted by red metal pennants decorated with three white stars.

Eventually, like the canal boats, the trams proved too slow for modern travelers. After World War II, Nai Lert, a local entrepreneur, introduced two bus lines and the popularity of the trams began to wane. In 1965, the tram bell was silenced as the last coach was retired from service. Soon after, road workers poured asphalt over the rails, smothering their screeching forever.

—*Thanks to Valentine Egereff who forsook his native Russia in the 1930s and until his death in the 1970s made Bangkok his home.*

Nonetheless the water-borne and other vector diseases which had always cut such a terrifying swath through the populace, were largely a thing of the past, thanks to refrigeration, septic tanks, insecticides, public comprehension of germ theory, inoculations, antibiotics, and a general improvement in home sanitation.

In short, what we see in these photographs — as in any photograph — is the visible, the static, the silent. What we do not see is any sign of tension or chaos or of hidden killers. We don't smell the streets, feel the heat, hear the babble and the din. Thus, the photographs only partially represent the setting into which the expatriates of a century ago stepped, unprepared by television, magazines, or any of the other media available to us today before we brave a foreign clime.

Descendents of the voluptuously-shaped Iamjun *barges that brought fresh water to soothe parched throats during the hot season lie at anchor in the Chao Phya River. Today, they transfer cargo from large ships to the wharves.*

ones they used for sewage and garbage disposal — which helps explain the virulence of cholera and other water-borne disease epidemics. Recognizing a need for potable water for his subjects, King Chulalongkorn near the end of his reign initiated the construction of a water purification system. Still under construction when he died in 1910, fresh water flowed from the first tap only in 1914.

Sanitation, or the lack thereof, was clearly a major problem. Carter, in 1904, reported that there were 79 public latrines with a total of 361 compartments.[7] Klongs were still used as sewers despite King Mongkut's public admonition in his charming 1858 edict, "On the Inelegant Practice of Throwing Dead Animals into the Waterways."

In 1999, the rivers and canals were still badly polluted, and Bangkok's public sewage system was still under construction.

> The Tramways Co. Ltd., seem to have decided to leave their hard-driving conductors to the tender mercies of the law. This is a complete change in the policy of this autocratic street railway company. Just twelve years ago, one of the company's cars ran over a little girl at Pratoo Sam Yot, killing her outright, and on that occasion the *Bangkok Times* ventured to remark that the driver, one Nai Won was — well, not a member of the Blue Ribbon army [a temperance organization].
>
> Forthwith, the company instructed counsel and went to all sorts of expense in prosecuting this paper with the result that we were mulcted in 150 ticals for daring to impugn the character of a tramcar driver. The judgement was notoriously unjust but that was not surprising in those days; and if we remember rightly half of Bangkok were called to say that they had never seen Nai Won the worse for liquor.
>
> Now, however, the management of the company has come to recognise that the employees are not quite perfect, but it will not be an easy thing to convince these men that the streets of Bangkok were not specially constructed as a race course for their cars. Among their latest little pleasantries they have succeeded in 'knocking spots' out of a carriage in which Messrs. Roberts and Tartas were seated and have upset the person and conveyance of Mr. Lawson [the police chief].
>
> —March 1900

To provide Bangkok citizens with clean drinking water, King Chulalongkorn began construction of the Bangkok Waterworks at the corner of Bamrungmuang and Worachak Roads a facility that was not completed until November 27, 1914, four years after his death. In the old days, a canal ran alongside one side of the waterworks. Across it, H.R.H. Prince Bhanurangsi Sawangwongse, owner of Wang Burapha (Burapha Palace), built a bridge which he painted black in memory of his deceased wife and son. Its name, Saphan Dam (Black Bridge), became that of the surrounding district. Each end of the bridge was ornamented with the heads of two oxen. In each ox's nose was a brass ring fitted with a chain from which dangled a small metal cup. When a thirsty passerby pressed the ox's nose, water would gush forth to be caught in the cup.

Rain water costs a *salung* (25 *satang*) per two tins in Bangkok at present. It seems a moderate price if the water is good but it seems a very great deal to those who are in the greatest need of it. Of course, the water supplied from the Royal Navy boats is still free but Bangkok is too scattered a town to be supplied by two boats.

—April 1900

Note: During the hot season, before the completion of the waterworks, barges traveled up the Chao Phya River to be filled with fresh river water which would then be sold to Bangkok residents.

LIVING IN BANGKOK AT THE BEGINNING OF THE TWENTIETH CENTURY

In 1904, J.G.D. Campbell, a businessman and an experienced observer with an astute eye recorded his impressions of Bangkok in this manner:

"The expectant visitor, after sailing up twenty-five miles of the broad and stately Menam, will probably derive much disappointment from his first experience of Bangkok. His earliest acquaintance will most probably be with a long, dingy, squalid road [New Road], running for several miles parallel with the river, and connecting the mercantile quarter with the old walled city, a road lined on both sides with third-rate Chinese shops, and thronged with Asiatics of every hue and costume, a perfect bedlam of coolies, rickshaws, carriages, bicycles, and that culmination of modern civilisation, electric trams...

"To those who do not simply carry their own habits and customs about wherever they go, and who feel the charm of the freshness and novelty of a new life and surroundings, Bangkok will offer no little attraction...It has one advantage, perhaps, over many of the other big towns of the East...it affords a more varied and interesting society than is to be found in, at any rate, the big colonial capitals of the British Empire. But this point of superiority apart, existence is dull and limited, it must be admitted, from the strictly Western aspect. There are the usual recreations of lawn tennis, golf, bicycling, riding and racing, which are always to be found wherever a certain number of Europeans are gathered together; but these are not of a very exciting nature, and gay ladies will miss the garden parties and the dances, the excursions and the picnics which help to pass time pleasantly in Singapore and Hong Kong.

"A great drawback to Bangkok, too, is the fact that there is no place for the jaded European to go to for a few days' change There are no hill stations up country. The only resorts are the island of Koh Si Chang in the Gulf of Siam and Anghin and Siracha on the eastern shore. But at none of these is there any hotel, and those who wish to get the benefit of the sea breezes can only do so at the inconvenience of carrying with them all their provisions and most of their furniture, not to mention servants."

—J.G.D. Campbell, *Siam in the Twentieth Century* [8]

Outer New Road as it looked in 1900, with shanties strung along the sides of the road and a tram track running along one lane.

The Bangkok Times.

ESTABLISHED, 1887.

ESTABLISHED, 1887.

VOL. XXII.   SATURDAY, 3RD FEBRUARY, 1900.   วัน เสาร์ ที่ ๓ กุมภาพันธ์ รัตน โกสินทรศก ๑๑๘   No: 19576.

64

OUR WINDOW ON AN ANTIQUE AGE

Most history books take a lofty perspective on an age, providing a broad summation of larger events. Few texts document the details of daily life, the mundane background against which those larger events play. But it is the stories of everyday life which are the most interesting, the most human to readers today. They give us a view of society from the ground level shared by the common man, the status most of us occupy. Such perspective allows us to compare our fears and delights with those of people long since gone.

For a human perspective for the year 1900 in Bangkok, we must read the newspapers of the day. They provide us with an idea of the issues that occupied most expatriates' time and thoughts. The most popular English-language newspaper was the *Bangkok Times*. Its editions of 1900 and 1901 are the source of the 120-plus news items placed around this book.

Left: The front page of the February 3, 1900 edition of the Bangkok Times *was filled with shipping news and advertisements; news began on Page Two. Right: The* Bangkok Daily Mail, *a Thai-language daily, was founded by King Vajiravudh. Its office on Siphya Road, was inundated in the flood of 1917.*

LETTER TO THE EDITOR
Dear Sir,
    In Saturday's issue of the *Siam Free Press* there appeared under the heading of "A Suicide's Confession" a statement to the effect that I had committed suicide and that "a twinge of remorse was unaccountable for it." I shall feel exceedingly obliged if you will correct this very grievous mistake since I have not departed this life under the disturbing circumstances related by the *Siam Free Press* but that it was my valuable servant, a lad named Nai Yee, with whom I would not have parted for anything who took his life, much to my regret and that of a wide circle of his friends by whom he was held in the greatest esteem for his integrity and honesty.
    I shall feel greatly obliged if you will publish this letter in the columns of your esteemed journal. I remain, Sir,
                Yours truly, Chamun Maha Sanit.

(Reply) Our contemporary has already apologised for the mistake made but in the circumstances a man seems to have a right to be allowed to proclaim his existence as widely as possible. — Editor.
                —December 1900

The following is typical of many of the so-called editorials in the Times.

WHY WE SIT ON TABLES

About ten million women are exasperated every day by men sitting on tables. So far as I am aware, women do not pay for the furniture and it is none of their business how it is used. The habit of men sitting on tables had led to the invention of the cushioned billiard table and will no doubt ultimately result in other clever notions.

At one time, it was supposed that men sat on tables to exercise without exertion by swinging their legs and by kicking the legs of the table. The scientific fact is that tables are more magnetic than chairs. If three men walk into a room where there is no woman, two of them will make for the table.

The source of this magnetism is the friction that women create by polishing tables frequently. Of course, women say that they only polish tables because men sit on them and spoil them but this is illogical and feminine. No really clever men sit on chairs. They use their chairs for keeping their papers and things on, also their feet.

Chairs are notoriously immoral. You will notice that when a well-bred man loses his temper, invariably he gets up from his chair and makes a direct line for the nearest table. This enables him to keep his temper and to argue reasonably. The importance of tables for this purpose has long been recognised by furniture-makers. You will notice that the tables in a billiard room, which is essentially a man's room, are always supplied with eight stubby, substantial legs. On the other hand, a woman's davenport or the knickpack tables in her boudoir have thin and spidery legs that are no use for sitting on. From this it might be argued that women never sit on tables. The man who takes the trouble to investigate, however, will find out that they do so in secret.

Every morning after breakfast, the lady of the house retreats into the back quarters on what she calls "household duties". Her real object is to go down to the servants' room and sit on the kitchen table under the pretence of ordering dinner. It is quite time that the uselessness and impropriety of chairs should be recognised. If people only sat on tables and on window ledges and on the edges of beds, the world would be a great deal happier.

—May 1900

Bangkok's first newspaper in any language appeared in the decade following the re-opening of Thailand to the West. In 1844, Dr. D.B. Bradley, an American Presbyterian minister, founded a weekly printed in Thai. Unfortunately, it lasted only one year, felled by the lack of a proper distribution system.

In 1864, Mr. J.H. Chandler published an English-language weekly called the *Bangkok Times* which also lasted for only a year, put out of business by a successful libel suit brought by an irate reader. The *Bangkok Recorder*, also published in English, suffered the same ignoble fate but was revived as a Thai language periodical, although

> In February, we sent out our usual little reminders for accounts owing for subscriptions to the *Bangkok Times*. Although dispatched about the 14th, they were not intended as Valentines.
> —February 1901

even that ultimately failed due to lack of interest. Both papers must have been somewhat scurrilous if we can accept the implications of a contemporary observation: "Bangkok was left for two years in the Arcadian-like and peaceful condition of being without a newspaper of any description."

The revived *Bangkok Times* hit the streets in 1887, this time published by T. Lloyd-Williamese at his printing office on New Road near Siphya Road. Initially issued as a weekly, the paper became so

> We have a received a visit from Mr. G.M. Schilling, an American who says he is walking round the world for a wager; and one of the conditions of it is that he must not pay for anything. We have heard that yarn before and we have seen lots of people who do not pay. Usually, they do not walk, either.
> —February 1901

popular that it soon appeared bi-weekly. Its success spawned a competitor in the *Siam Free Press*, born in 1891. Although written in English, the *Free Press* featured stories of interest primarily to the city's French community. The pages of the *Bangkok Times* abound with swipes at its upstart rival, seen as a mouthpiece for the French

In 1900, the Siphya Cross—the intersection of New Road and Siphya Road—was one of the most important commercial crossroads in the city. Its most important landmark was Kiam Hoa Heng, a leading dry good stores that had several branches scattered through various districts. On down the street on the right were the offices of the Bangkok Times *newspaper. While everything else has disappeared, the building on the left has survived virtually unchanged.*

A new law published in the latest *Gazette* brings Siam into line with Western nations in the matter of copyright. The preamble points out that, hitherto, authors have had no protection for their work in this country. Anyone had the right to republish and sell any book.

The new enactment follows the lines of the English law, giving protection for 42 years, or the period of the author's life with a grace of seven years, whichever is the longer.

As trade bulks so very much larger than letters in modern Siam, it is to be trusted that the Government will without delay follow up this law with another giving protection to trademarks.

—September 1901

government, with which Britain was tussling for preeminence in Thailand. Colonial ambitions were still very much alive throughout Asia, and the *Times'* editors enthusiastically scoffed at French

diplomatic initiatives and the mapping surveys being conducted by the Pavie Commission with the intent to establish Thailand's borders. The nationalistic broadsides were a free-for-all that titillated both papers' readers.

In 1903, the *Siam Observer*, made its appearance. Wright and Breakspear note that none of the papers approached news impartially: "The papers now work in complete harmony with the Government; they are generally kept well posted with official news, and it is an open

Societé Anonyme Belge was the city's leading retailer of fine jewelry. In the 1920s, it moved to this handsome new building at the corner of New Road and Worachak Road. The premises are now the home of Sing Sian Yit Pao, a leading Chinese-language newspaper.

secret that they receive Government subsidies." [9] This connivance, more than any factor ensured that the papers would not be shut down by lawsuits. It also laid the groundwork for a policy of 'prior restraint' or self-censorship that has guided newspaper editors through much of the 20th century. As shown by many of the news items that appear in this book, however, the reporters were not entirely restrained in their editorializing.

In 1900, the *Bangkok Times*, by now a six-page broadsheet, enjoyed the largest circulation. It appeared each evening, Monday through Saturday and while it was ostensibly an information source, fully three-quarters of each issue was devoted to advertisements. In fact, not a single news item appeared on the front page, which was devoted to small ads the size of today's Classifieds.

Most foreign news came via Reuter's Telegrams, often many days after the event and often out of sequence. Strongly British in flavor, the *Times*' big overseas stories in 1900 were the Boer War in South Africa, the Chinese Emperor's health, and the Boxer Rebellion in 'Peiping'. In 1901 the two earthshaking events were the assassination

Evidence that a portion of the readership of English-language newspapers was Thai can be assumed from the fact that the papers carried advertisements in two languages. In this instance, one can presume that Thais were as avid as Europeans in riding new-fangled bicycles.

SIAM IN THE HOME PRESS.
The *Black and White Budget* of the 13th ultimate [i.e. last month] contains a picture showing "the King of Siam taking his usual morning constitutional." His Majesty, in an overcoat, knee breeches and putties, is riding a camel and the other chief figure in the picture is an Arab in his white robes. That does not strike as being quite the familiar sight here that the *Black and White Budget* seems to suppose. Presumably it is from a photograph taken in Egypt, but was supposed in London to show the King of Siam at home.
Then, here is another amazing thing from a home paper, the *Globe*. Perhaps Sunadalaya College is meant to be referred to, but it is not easy to guess what is meant by such nonsense. "A somewhat curious school has been opened at Bangkok by an English lady. The pupils are fifteen in

number, and they are all princesses of the Royal family of Siam. They are taught to do everything that a good housekeeper should do. They cook, wash clothes, bake, sweep the rooms, lay the table, arrange the flowers, and, in short, learn to make themselves generally useful. They leave the school to be married at the age of fifteen and it is said that a Siamese Princess now makes an admirable wife."

—May 1901

Note: Sunandalaya College was a girls' school established to commemorate the tragic drowning of King Chulalongkorn's Queen, Sunanda, and her baby at Bang Pa-in. It sat at the mouth of Klong Talat and later was incorporated into Rajini School, established by her sister, Queen Saowapha.

of U.S. President McKinley and the death of Queen Victoria. Major stories were augmented by items gleaned and re-written from the pages of other regional papers as well as from newspapers and periodicals arriving by steamship from Europe and North America. Entertainment pure and simple was the newspaper's mainstay with oddities featured prominently. Many items masquerading as the absolute truth could only have been written tongue in cheek.

Thailand news was compiled by local reporters. While stories about the monarchy, affairs of state, and commerce were treated with dutiful respect, there was a liberal sprinkling of pieces on local personalities, business events, and the community's — or the paper's — pet projects and peeves, and there was no shortage of complaints among the foreigners who wrote for and to the newspapers. Although sedate in approach, the stories were characterized as much by personal commentary and shoot-from-the-shoulder editorializing as by hard facts.

Interlarding the serious stories was a wealth of lighter stories — light to the point of frivolity — designed to amuse its foreign readers. Such stories, usually commenting on the common man's foibles, were less than culturally sensitive and far from politically correct by latter day standards but are at least partly explainable by the frustrations of living in a strange land far from home.

A far cry from a cubicle in an air-conditioned glass complex, yesterday's business offices were ill-lit and cooled by fans. Those offices located along the Chao Phya would have benefitted from river breezes but even on the best of days afternoons must have been sweltering and productivity between noon and 4 p.m. must have been minimal.

THE EUROPEAN QUARTER

In 1900 most of the men among Bangkok's 1,000 expatriate residents were engaged in a wide variety of white collar jobs. Many Europeans and North Americans were employed as officials at the dozen foreign legations located in the 'European' section of the city, roughly the area bounded by Siphya and Sathorn Roads, and lying between the river and New Road. Other foreign experts and administrators had been invited by King Chulalongkorn to serve as advisors to Thai government departments, while still others worked for foreign mercantile or shipping companies. A few established law and medical practices, or were proprietors of small specialty stores selling European goods. Missionaries proselytized their faith to the

TO THE EDITOR

Can you or any of your readers kindly inform me whether Tapioca has been systemically cultivated in this country, and if so, with what results? Any information on this subject will greatly oblige.

Yours truly, Sago

Reply: We have no information to give our correspondent about the cultivation of tapioca in Siam. But very few cultivators take up anything except paddy seriously and it is to be hoped the Agricultural Department will in due course succeed in encouraging the cultivation of many other plants. An attempt is at present being made to cultivate rubber plants here.

—March 1900

Note: By the mid-1970s, Thailand would be the world's number one exporter of tapioca, supplying fully 95 percent of the tapioca for the animal feed markets of Europe. Similarly, it would become the world's third largest exporter of natural rubber.

At the turn of the century, Bangkok held nearly as many banking firms as there were nationalities living in Thailand. They ranged from branches of major international houses that provided investment funds to burgeoning businesses, to small local institutions that had begun their lives as backstreet moneylenders. The Credit Foncier de l'Indochine (above) was a prominent French bank in the European quarter.

'unbelievers' in what surely must have been a frustrating endeavor; records show they made few converts, Thai Buddhism being a vigorous, and more comfortable, faith.

Many of the Westerners had been seconded by their own governments to aid the Siamese government in its reorganization and modernization. Several of them headed departments. The Siamese Navy, for example, was commanded by a Dane, Admiral Richlieu. Mr. W.A.G. Tilleke was the Acting Attorney-General of Siam. A Dutchman, Homan van der Heide, oversaw irrigation and canal development in the provinces, and Lt. Colonel Gerini headed the Royal Military College. Many other foreigners were involved in financial administration, infrastructure development, and commercial relations, all of them working under a Thai minister or department head.

Left: The Hong Kong and Shanghai Bank opened for business in Bangkok in 1888, and in 1890 moved into this handsome building, once a landmark at the entrance to Klong Padung Krung Kasem. In 1977, it moved its headquarters to Siam Center but before the building was pulled down, it served as the fictional U.S. Embassy in the movie 'The Deerhunter'. Top left: Shortly after it was demolished, the Royal Orchid Sheraton Hotel was erected on the site, opening its doors to guests in 1982, Bangkok's Bicentennial year. On the canal's opposite bank, River City Shopping Center was built.

AN EDITORIAL

What came we out for to see? The European community in a Far Eastern port like Bangkok did not come out to see Siamese life and customs but it is at least peculiar how little interest we take in the life of the people around us. Our own home ways we rigidly enforce in our own little circle till these have come to rigidly hedge us in. Of Siamese ways the ordinary *farang* knows really next to nothing. We go to elaborate Siamese entertainments given by one or other of the Government departments and there we find few Siamese while the whole entertainment is conducted on purely European lines.

—February 1900

Above right: Trees are no longer harvested in northern Thai forests; today, logs are imported from Burma and Cambodia, dropped in the rivers, and floated to the sawmills. In the old days, elephants muscled them to the banks of rivers like the Ping, Yom, Wang, and Nan where they floated downstream into the river they fed, the Chao Phya. Today, while trucks have taken over the role once performed by elephants, the methods of rafting logs in Nakhon Sawan and towing them downriver to Bangkok sawmills has not changed over the century. Here, having completed their long journey downstream, the rafts wait along the riverbank above Bangkok, Right: Grahlert was one of the preeminent jewelers of the period, the kruut *(garuda) and elaborate symbols decorating its premises denoting royal patronage. It sat on Tanao Road at the head of a small lane called Soi Chang Thong, or 'Goldsmith Lane'.*

Above left: This corner of Rajdamnern Avenue has experienced a number of incarnations in the past century. Badman's Department Store, a turn of the century landmark located just west of the present Lottery Bureau at the Phanpipopleela Bridge, was transformed into the Law School in the 1920s, and then on May 3, 1933, it became the Publicity Division. Below left: In 1946, it was still standing, opposite the Royal Hotel, but it was eventually demolished and a new building was later erected to house the Public Relations Department. That building was badly damaged by fire during the insurrection of October 14, 1973 and was later pulled down. The widening of the approaches to Rajdamnern has obliterated the site. Khao Sarn Road, a street of backpacker hotels, parallels Rajdamnern just to the north. Below: A rival firm, the John Sampson and Son furniture store at Pan Fah was built on a triangle of land formerly occupied by several gambling houses. The most popular was Ban Ton Makam (Tamarind Gambling House) where cockfights were the special attraction. Sampsons' ceased business in the 1920s and its former premises now houses the Public Works Department.

A number of Europeans worked for joint venture companies buying and exporting teak logs. The enterprise dated from the 1860s but grew rapidly after 1873 when tropical hardwoods found favor in overseas markets. By 1900 teak was big business, earning both the government and concessionaires huge sums of money. Cut in the north, the trees were then floated downriver to dozens of sawmills located in Bangkok. Many of the mills, occupying the riverbanks between Nonthaburi and the Krung Thon Bridge, still cut timber from logs floated down from Nakhon Sawan.

Several of the city's department stores were foreign-owned. One of the most famous was Harry A. Badman & Co., established on January 1, 1884 near the Royal Barracks (next to the present Lottery Bureau at the corner of Rajdamnern Avenue and Chakkrapong Road). Patronized by Thai royalty it was known to shoppers and postal authorities as 'No. 1, Bangkok'. Another department store, John Sampson and Son, occupied a handsome colonial-style building at Pan Fah that now serves as the offices of the Public Works Department. Falck, already mentioned in connection with hotels, seems to have been an enterprising man because with his partner, he had formed Falck and

Above: Department stores imported the latest American and European fashions which were quickly snapped up by Bangkok's foreign and Thai ladies or were replicated by the city's talented dressmakers. Unchanged over the century are the dictates of fashion over practicality. While men wore long coats and top hats, women chose long dresses, both of them wholly inappropriate in a Bangkok before air-conditioning. Left: The Oriental Bakery stocked European breads and pastries, baked fresh daily.

Beidek in 1878. He must have been spectacularly successful because by 1905, he had built an imposing three-story store which is now the home of the Oriental Place shopping center.

Foreigners enjoyed special privileges in Thailand, a status granted by a Thai leadership well aware of the colonial servitude of neighbor states which had failed to bow to the Europeans' self-conceived superiority. At the heart of the system was the concept of extra-territoriality. Insisted upon by each treaty power, extra-territoriality meant that any foreigner accused of a crime would not be tried in a Thai court, but rather in a consular court presided over by a magistrate of his own nationality. As a result, there were ten consular courts in Bangkok, each having a unique procedure and a different system of law.

Foreign wives occupied themselves with running their large households, which meant directing small armies of servants. The ladies also attended teas and paid social calls on their neighbors; in the absence of telephones, they would send a servant ahead with a calling card to announce an intended visit. Life was hard and the everyday difficulties were made more challenging by the perils of giving birth and raising children in unsanitary conditions. Headstones in cemeteries dating from this period attest to lives foreshortened by disease.

As tourism on any scale was still 20 years away, most foreign strangers walking the streets were probably sailors on shore leave. Newspaper accounts suggest that they were a raffish lot, much given to drinking and brawling.

Above left: Although many foreigners worked in the employ of the Thai government, the ministries were headed by Thais, who were also beginning to assume wider roles in business. Left: Quite early in the century, Thai lawyers began taking the place of Europeans in adjudicating the law. Here, Thai law students prepare for the bar in the newly-revised judicial system.

LIFESTYLES

Well-to-do European families lived in several widely-spaced neighborhoods: Bangkolem (at the lower end of New Road), along Suriwongse Road, Sathorn Road, and in Sapatoom. The latter was dominated by Wat Patoomawanaram and the Sapatoom Palace — until her passing, the home of His Majesty King Bhumibol's mother — located behind Siam Center on Rama I Road.

They occupied homes that were by this point being built in the European style, offering spacious rooms, livery stables for horses and carriages, a kitchen — generally set well away from the house to keep the odors and the noise of cooking from invading the living areas — servants' quarters, and other outbuildings. Most European and Thai nobles' homes had spacious gardens where families relaxed and guests

> It is hoped that, under the rules of the new municipality, the *farang* who leaves a whining pup tied up in his house will be shot.
> —January 1900

Until his tragic death in 1895, this was the home of Somdet Chao Fa Maha Vajirunahis, the Crown Prince of Thailand. Called, in English, 'Old Windsor Palace', it was demolished to build the National Stadium on Rama I Road. 'Sapatoom', the area in which it sat, means 'Lotus Pond' and referred to a large, lotus-filled lake (now earth-filled) near Wat Pathoomawanaram, which sits just to the east of the Siam Intercontinental Hotel.

The Victory Monument was built in 1941 to celebrate triumph in a brief 1939 territorial skirmish with France that took place in Laos. Dominating the intersection of Phya Thai and Rajavithi Roads, the monument once marked the northern boundary of the Sapatoom enclave containing houses occupied by prosperous Europeans and Thais. When this photograph was taken in 1946, it still demarcated the northern extremity of urban development. Beyond it, Paholyothin, the extension of Phya Thai Road ran through a rural area with a few houses sitting amidst rice fields. Today, the monument marks the lower end of a vast residential, industrial, and office district that extends virtually to Don Muang Airport 20 kilometers to the north. It also hosts a daily traffic jam that may see diminuation once the Skytrain — inaugurated in December 1999 — gains popularity among the commuting public.

The building operations now going on along Sapatoom Road (Rama I) may be taken as evidence that the Government recognizes the advantage of investing capital in house property for the purpose of comfortably accommodating its employees. Some of them live rent free while others pay a moderate rental out of a special allowance made to them and they are thus saved from having to pay the absurd rents extorted in the lower part of the town.

Besides, the Rue Belge, as it used to be called, is becoming a more aristocratic quarter than ever, and property there is steadily appreciating in value.

But with the constant increase in the number of residents the pressure caused by the want of good house property in Bangkok does not become less. Suriwong Road grows, of course, but only very slowly, and no landlords are eager to invest their money in providing house accommodation for the *farang*. The fact is that if a row of small cheap wooden houses is run up in the space occupied by one ordinary cottage residence, they pay very much better.

But it is farther north than even Sapatoom Road that the best residential quarter of Bangkok will be found [Paholyothin Road], probably in the comparatively near future. The enormous improvements that have been effected in the Dusit Park neighborhood are bound to attract all who are able to fix their residence and already there are quite a number of very big houses completed in that quarter.

—February 1900

were entertained. For soirees, female guests were provided with cloth bags in which they encased their feet, the fabric serving to keep mosquitoes from feasting on their ankles.

Households ran smoothly thanks to a multitude of servants employed by both Thai and European families. Whereas today, having a servant is a novelty for foreigners used to running their households by themselves, for Europeans of the age, it was simply the substitution

of one nationality of servants for another. Until World War I erupted in Europe — and before factory employment began drawing them away in large numbers — servants comprised one-sixth of the work force; by contemporary definition a 'lower middle class' household was one that employed fewer than three servants. Coping with them in Bangkok in an age when few Thais spoke English meant that is was essential that Europeans learn to speak Thai or risk courting chaos on a daily basis.

In an age before refrigeration, produce was brought into the house each day. Blocks of ice delivered to the door cooled food, which was cooked over a charcoal fire. Without screened windows, insects were constant invaders. The leg of virtually every table and cabinet was set in a cup of water, a mini-moat that kept ants and other crawling insects from taking over a house and destroying the larder.

A home was regarded as a refuge from the outside world, a haven of peace in which to raise a family. One entertained guests in one's home. Announcements appeared in newspapers noting that "Mrs. Smith will be at home from 2 to 4 p.m. Tuesday next", an indication that the lady of the manor was keeping an open house to which one could pay a visit without prior invitation.

Foreign bachelors resided in European-managed hotels which doubled as serviced apartments. Hotels had been a feature of the city's

---

A resident who has had old memories stirred by a letter in the Siam Observer today on the history of Windmill Road [Silom] sends us the following:

The road was made in the time of the late King (Mongkut), I believe at the request of Sir T.G. Knox and in those early days the greatest care was taken that the cattle traders should not monopolize it.

Their cattle were only allowed to pass single file in order that it might not be cut up. Barrot, a French cattle trader, used to give much trouble and he was arrested again and again for cutting the road up.

It was considered so important a road that Mr. Newman of the British Consulate has instructions to exercise a general supervision over it. When Sir Thomas Knox took his rides morning and evening along it, the Klings [a southern Indian ethnic group who worked as cattle herders] were wary of meeting him. They all disappeared as soon as he turned the corner at the bridge (at New Road). The *klong* was dug somewhere in 1864 or '65 but cattle boats were not allowed to be kept in it. The cattle were landed at Sapatoom [Bobae Market].
—September 1900

landscape since the 1830s when Siam re-opened its doors to foreign traders. In 1864 the charmingly named 'Cottage Home', located near the present Oriental Hotel, was managed by one Charles Thomas and catered primarily to foreign sailors. An 1869 edition of the *Bangkok Recorder* noted the birth of a child at the nearby Falck's Hotel. As implied by its full name — Falck's Bowling Alley and Billiard Hall — Falck's was an entertainment hall that also offered boarding and lodging. During the rainy season, it must have been subject to flooding from the nearby river because the structure is described as a

By the 1920s, houses designed along European lines with spacious gardens, separate kitchens and servants' quarters were being built for resident foreigners as well as for Thai nobles and wealthy businessmen. At this point, the livery stables for horses and carriages had been consigned to history and four wheels had been assigned to occupy the space formerly utilized by four hooves.

long, low, one-story building raised on piles about four feet high.

Falck's appears to have been at the epicenter of the hotel district with most inns clustered around New Road between Siphya and Silom roads. We know that the Kross Hotel, location unknown, was expanded in 1888 because an announcement stated that, "The

Right: The parlor of a European house was cooled by fans and featured wicker furniture of local manufacture. Note the many photographs of relatives left behind at home. Below: The living room in an age before air-conditioning when a ceiling fan stirred torpid air into the semblance of a breeze. Below right: The dining room with the table set for guests.

Below: While one hopes that the name of this hotel on Klong Padung Krung Kasem near the Paknam Railway Station — and later the Hualampong Railway Station — was meant to be 'Novel' or 'Royal' Hotel rather than the unfortunate 'Hovel' printed on it, the latter word would seem to describe the hosteleries discussed by early travelers to Bangkok. Many other hotels would appear as the popularity of the railways brought more travelers to Thailand.

building makes no pretensions to grandeur...but all those of a quiet and frugal nature will find cleanliness, comfort and civility at Mr. Kross' establishment".

From contemporary accounts Kross's and a few others appear to have been the exceptions to the rule. Hotels were generally regarded as inadequate in number and substandard. In 1897 Maxwell Sommerville wrote that, "The reader, who is possibly on his way to Siam, may esteem himself fortunate should the manager be able to accommodate him, for Siam is not a land of hotels." [10]

HRH Crown Prince Maha Vajiravudh, who became king in 1910, made the point even more forcefully in a letter to a London

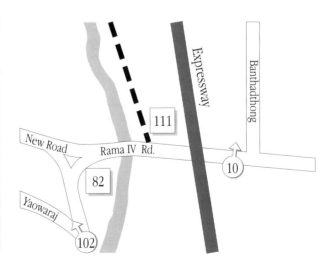

Below: The curved building in the left picture was the An An, one of the premier hotels in Chinatown. Situated at the eastern end of Yaowaraj Road, it underwent several renovations before emerging in the 1950s in its present form as the substantially reduced New Empire Hotel. Right: The Oriental Hotel dining room in 1900.

83

In 1900, the Oriental Hotel behind the trees on the left, the East Asiatic Company offices, and the Chartered Bank Building at far right were the tallest structures on the riverbank. Today, they are dwarfed by office buildings along Silom Road and New Road. Of the trio of buildings, The Oriental and the East Asiatic Company premises continue to serve their former functions but the Chartered Bank offices are now an assembly hall for the Assumption School, another long-time riverbank resident and a reminder of the old days.

friend: "I might also warn you that our hotels are really disgusting. There is no other word for it. The King's Privy Purse department, I hear, are arranging with a certain C.G. Edwards, an American commercial man well-known here to build for him an up-to-date hotel. But until this is finished, I would not advise you to trust yourselves to any of the hotels in Bangkok."

Things had improved considerably by 1900 with several hotels enjoying prominence. Among them, The Oriental (founded in 1876), Hotel d'Europe, Hotel de la Paix, the Bristol, and the Palace were well on their way to becoming the city's leading social and residential establishments.

84

FEARS AND CONCERNS

Aside from the privileges they enjoyed — luxurious homes, servants to cater to every need, lavish parties, etc. — foreigners' lives were far from idyllic. The torrid climate was quite unlike the frigid winters of their home countries. Expatriates dwelt far from relatives, aware that if anything adverse were to happen to loved ones at home, there was little they could do to help. When they waved goodbye from the decks of ships carrying them to Siam, they knew that they might be seeing friends and relations for the last time.

Like their Thai hosts and friends, foreigners were constantly reminded of the fragility of life. In an age before sanitation, and before vaccines and antibiotics that could stay death's hand, tropical diseases threatened constantly; even a small cut could result in death. Knowing the perils that awaited them, their resoluteness in venturing forth to an alien, hostile land is laudable. While hygienic standards might not

> There have been five deaths from smallpox in Windmill Road [Silom] in the past four days and there are at present at least a dozen more cases of smallpox now in the same street. The majority of those attacked are children. There is also one case of cholera. Bangkok is, of course, never free from smallpox but at present there seems to be something of an epidemic.
>
> —January 1900

have been much better in their home countries, foreigners were aware that the tropics held terrible diseases that struck with disturbing frequency. Even the Thais were not immune to these maladies. King Chulalongkorn, the Lord of Life, had watched helplessly as his son, Crown Prince Maha Vajirunahis, caught a cold and died of complications at age 17 on January 4, 1895.

Canals like Klong Banglamphu — here, after intersecting with Klong Makkasan running to the left, its name changes to Klong Ong Ang--served as the city's sewers and thus were sources of disease. On their deaths, cholera victims were carried for cremation to the courtyard of Wat Saket, situated at the base of Phu Khao Thong (Golden Mount) in the background of this early 20th century photo. Built to its present height in the reign of Rama IV, Phu Khao Thong was erected to replicate an artificial mountain of the same name just outside of Ayutthaya. Until 1957, its sides were covered in trees and vines but erosion threats to its soft soil led planners to clad it in concrete.

The lack of clean drinking water was compounded by concern about the safety of milk. In 1903 Wright and Breakspear noted that, "Some years ago an exhaustive inspection and inquiry was made into the milk supply, and the conditions were found so bad that all dairies were removed to grazing ground supplied by the Siamese Government on the outskirts of the town at Klong Toi." [11]

There were mosquito-borne diseases like breakbone fever (dengue), hemorrhagic fever, malaria, and the so-called blackwater fever (debilitation resulting from repeated malarial attacks). Contaminated food could cause dysentery, giardia, or tropical sprue so virulent the victims often wasted away in days. Lice brought typhus,

Below: Sampeng Lane's closeness made it a breeding ground for contagions.

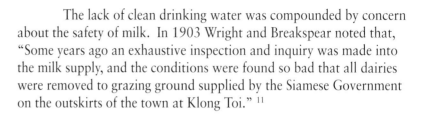

As a precaution in times of cholera, Messrs. B. Grimm and Co. strongly recommend their 'Securitas' which renders the body capable of throwing off infection. It also kills the microbes in the water to which it imparts a refreshing taste so that 'Securitas' should be of the greatest value at the present season. B. Grimm and Co.'s cholera mixture has been a well-known remedy for more than a quarter of a century.
—April 1900

Note: The April editions of the *Bangkok Times* were filled with obituaries for Europeans who had died of cholera. It was not unusual that one day's notice of the death of a child (or children) would be followed the next day by news of the mother's death and day after by that of the father. The articles reflect a sense of grim resignation to the inevitable; something one awaited each hot season and from which he prayed he and his family would be spared.

dogs were rabid, milk transmitted tuberculosis, poor nutrition led to beri-beri and rickets, and the water often carried hepatitis, typhoid fever, cholera, and a dozen other killers including the most dreaded scourge of all, the disfiguring smallpox. Plague was still rampant in Bangkok, and 21 cases reported in 1907 resulted in nine deaths. Further, they were assailed by an array of skin diseases — undoubtedly exacerbated by the heavy clothes insisted upon by European decorum — such as scabies and shingles, and the non-fatal but maddening prickly heat. To prevent contagious diseases from entering the country, a quarantine facility at Koh Phra, an island 100 kilometers south of the Chao Phya River mouth, isolated immigrants, primarily Chinese laborers until they could be certified contagion-free by doctors.

We hear that the Britisher in Bangkok may once more die in peace undisturbed by the fear that on account of his nationality there will be no burial for him. The Consul and the undertaker are reported to have, well, 'buried the hatchet' seems the appropriate phrase. Moreover, a fixed tariff of fees has been agreed upon and you may now have a first, second, or third-class funeral.

—March 1901

The area near Ubolratana Bridge, where Pahurat Road crosses Klong Lawd, held several European dispensaries. The bridge, a modification of an older structure, was built in 1913 by King Vajiravudh as a cremation ceremony gift honoring Princess Ubolratana Nareenark, one of King Chulalongkorn's wives.

Cholera epidemics were especially feared. Cholera could turn the city into a charnel house, the disease insidiously creeping from home to home. The bodies of ordinary souls who died within the city walls were carried through the Pratu Phii (Spirit Gate) to be cremated at Wat Saket at the base of Phu Khao Thong (Golden Mount). Sometimes there were so many deaths that the corpses were simply laid out in the courtyards. Skies filled with the ominous black wings of vultures drawn by the carrion. It is easy to imagine the terror a mother felt to look out her window and see hundreds of the huge scavengers soaring in lazy circles, their shadows falling on the houses as they awaited their turn at the banquet table.

Fear of cholera inspired some novel nostrums of questionable efficacy. Newspapers admonished readers that, "The cholera belt

Above left: For Western pharmaceuticals, residents depended upon pharmacies like the Tha Tien Dispensary and the Seekak Phya Sri Dispensary. Left: The British Dispensary sat on New Road opposite Soi Rong Phasi (Customs House Lane). Note the Siamese flag, a white elephant on a red ground, the nation's symbol until World War II. Traditional herbal remedies were found at the Wat Po Herbal Medicine School, Thai homeopathic clinics, and apothecaries in Chinatown. Long before Western doctors recognized the benefits of Eastern medicine, Chinese pharmacists were dividing their shops down the middle; drawers with herbs and roots on one side, and shelves with Western medicines on the other, an arrangement which prevails today. Opposite page, top: In 1900, Siriraj Hospital was little more than a cluster of wooden buildings. It achieved prominence after Prince Mahidol of Songkhla, father of His Majesty King Bhumibol, returned to Thailand in the 1930s with his Harvard University medical degree, and began directing its modernization.

should always be worn when asleep in order to protect the abdominal organs from chill. In the tropics, the liver especially is in a continual state of engorgement, and it is the general experience of medical men in this climate that chills on the liver, stomach, and bowels form a very large percentage of all sicknesses to which Europeans and even natives are liable." [12]

> The last fatal case of cholera had its genesis in the aggressive durian. Thus is another charge brought against the fruit of fruits. It is not always referred to in this eulogistic manner but no matter.
> —May 1900

There was no shortage of medical advice dispensed by the newspapers. A typical article in the Bangkok Times states: "It is a well-known fact that the longer one stays in the tropics, the more one's 'nerves' seem to suffer. It will, therefore, be at once apparent that any condition suggesting instability of the nervous system, or any actual disease of the same, should contra-indicate one coming East…The presence of unsound teeth has been definitely proven to be the cause of pernicious anemia in temperate climates. In tropical climates any additional tendency to anemia should be avoided. Further, the inability to thoroughly masticate one's food is a serious drawback in Bangkok, where one has to tackle tough beef and tougher and drier fowls."

Another article warns, "Sleep, which is one of the greatest

> It has not yet been decided by scientists whether the sun really strikes through the back or through the head. But it has been discovered that a scarlet, orange or blue strip of flannel down the back and over the head gives absolute immunity from touches of sun.
> This is incidentally an argument in favour of the scarlet and blue 'jumpers' and if headgear were lined with material of either or all of these hues, the 'dangerous rays' of the sun would be effectually intercepted and dispersed before they could reach a vital spot.
> —December 1900

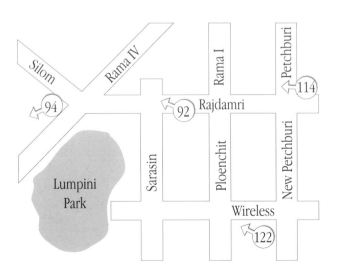

recuperative influences in the temperate climates, is even of greater value in the tropics. One really requires a fool's allowance in this climate. 'Early to bed and early to rise' is a golden rule, for the longer one lives in the tropics, the more one finds that late nights are a mistake." In 1999, such advice would fall on the deaf ears of late night revelers.

Yet another commentator advises, "A word in passing may be

said of cold baths. One should be careful not to overdo them, as over-indulgence brings about heart trouble, nervous prostration and liver complaints. So long as a cold bath is followed by a feeling of exhilaration and a glowing of the skin, the custom should be continued, but whenever a feel of chilliness or depression succeeds the cold tub, hot water should be used instead." Oddly, in their concern about chilling the body, Europeans did not follow the Chinese dictum that cold drinks shocked the internal organs and thus should be

Far left: Prominent in this 1946 photo south along Rajdamri Road are the twin water towers opposite Soi Sarasin. Above them was Chulalongkorn Hospital and the Saowapha Institute (Snake Farm) to the west; note the large number of canals. The Royal Bangkok Sports Club racetrack on the right and Lumpini Park on the left were being reburbished, the latter having served as a Japanese military encampment in World War II. Today, in a view from the top of Regent House, the dominent feature is the new Skytrain. Below: A view, farther south, of the King Rama VI Plaza on Rama IV Road opposite where the Dusit Thani Hotel and other gigantic buildings would rise after 1970.

shunned in favor of hot tea. Instead, on a hot afternoon, European men delighted in a gin or a stiff whiskey, cooled with ice made from boiled and filtered water.

A particularly plaintive warning counsels, "Funk [depression] during an epidemic of cholera should be avoided, for it is well known

Right: Until the 1970s, the Saladaeng area hemmed by Silom and Sathorn roads was prized for its bucholic atmosphere and the perception that the country air contributed to good health. Today, looking down from the roof of the Abdulrahim Tower on Rama IV Road near the Silom Road intersection towards Sathorn Road running across the top of the picture, the landmarks recognizable to a viewer in 1946 have all but disappeared. The mansion at center top of the older photo has been buried by the JUSMAG complex at the corner of Soi Atthakornprasit.

that fear kills a goodly percentage of those who fall in such an epidemic."

Foreigners of a more practical bent turned to prophylaxis and palliatives available at the city's numerous dispensaries. Many pharmacies, like the British Dispensary, doubled as clinics and offered the services of overseas doctors most of whom set up private practices and many of whom stayed to retire here.

In last resort, there were the hospitals. Like most Asians, Thais in the old days regarded hospitals as places where one went to

die after all remedies had failed, but foreigners retired to hospitals whenever illness struck. One such retreat, the Bangkok Nursing Home on the Sathorn Road end of Convent Road, was beautifully set amidst sheltering rain trees. Most Thais visited the government-funded hospitals at Bangrak and Samsen. Then, as now, the Police Hospital was the required destination for anyone injured as a result of a crime. Situated on Klong San in Thonburi, opposite the present-day River City Shopping Center, were the Hospital for Infectious Diseases

(Europeans called it the 'Plague Hospital') and, for those who succumbed to stress (or funk), the Asylum for the Insane (better known as the 'Lunatic Asylum').

Newspapers also devoted many column inches to crime and mayhem. It was the general feeling that each year's crop of immigrants brought a goodly number of professional criminals. There were also

POLICE BLOTTER FOR 1900, 1901

These, a sampling of the crimes reported by the Bangkok Times *in 1900 and 1901, are revealing both of the types of misdeeds as well as for the methods employed by the criminals.*

In the small hours of Wednesday morning a raid was made on the house of Nai Kum, at Klong Bang, at the end of Klong Bangkok Noi. Nai Kum and the inmates fled and the robbers, who found 524 *ticals*, went on their way rejoicing.

But Nemesis was on their track — and so was Nai Kum. Enlisting the assistance of the police, he came upon three of the thieves asleep in a house on Klong Mahasawat. On their faces was still the chalk affected by the Siamese robber when he goes a-robbing, and on one of the trio was found 120 *ticals* in silver.

The three are not thinking the matter out at Borisah Court No. 3 and Nai Kum is waxing important in the eyes of his neighbours.

—June 1901

On the north side of Klong Number 5 in Klong Rangsit district, 30 buffaloes belonging to one cultivator were stolen on the 15th of last month. The gang of thieves numbered some 13 men, most of them riding ponies.

The buffaloes were grazing about 10 *sen* [400 meters] from the owner's house. A herd of elephants proved something of an obstacle in the way of the thieves, but they succeeded in getting past and the owner of the buffaloes failed to catch them up.

These cattle robberies in the Klong Rangsit district are far too frequent and it is high time the Department responsible took more effective steps to make the robber's trade less ridiculously easy.

—March 1900

On Sunday evening a crowd of 30 or 40 men, principally sailors, were going round the streets of the town terrorizing everyone they met and making a collection of hats. The trouble had its origin at the fair of Wat Saket where they rescued a prisoner who was being taken to the lock-up and severely mauled the police constable.

Superintendent Miller heard of the party's peregrinations and traced them down Rachawong Road. The quarry was met in Yaowarat Road when a miniature charge was made by Mr. Miller and a head constable resulting in four arrests. The rest of the party cleared off into adjacent houses and passages but later in the evening, Chief Inspector Luang Atikorn and his assistants succeeded in arresting the whole of them. They were in possession of about 20 stolen hats which can now be seen at the Sam Yek Police Station.

—March 1900

About four o'clock on Monday morning, a Siamese was arrested in the street by the Bangkok police on the grounds that he was carrying a bundle with a loaded revolver, a couple of daggers, two braces and bits for boring and a number of charms such as burglars invariably take with them when going to commit a robbery. The only explanation he could give of his being in possession of such articles was that he had just bought them in a pawnshop and he was walking home.

The policeman thought that story a bit thin and took him to the station. The prisoner, however, is a *Mom Chao*, the son of the Prince and, according to the regulation defining the privileges of princes it seems that a *Mom Chao* cannot be put under arrest by the police or put on trial without special permission. That permission, we understand has been applied for and though we have not heard, we presume it has by this time been obtained.

The charge is a criminal one and the authorities can only support the police. Peers and princes have these privileges everywhere but these cannot save them from trial on criminal charges.

This particular *Mom Chao* has already served a sentence of ten years in gaol.

—August 1901

Another gang robbery is reported from the province of Pathumthani. Last Thursday morning some 20 buffaloes were being driven out to a field at Bang Toi when they were seized by a gang of 20 robbers. The head village men called out the people by drum and a number of shots were exchanged between the two parties.

The robbers fired off all their cartridges but they had the cattle and being the more numerous body succeeded in getting them away. The owners made up a party of ten and set off in pursuit coming up with the thieves somewhere near the border of Suphanburi province where another fight took place for the possession of the cattle.

The robbers having no cartridges were in danger of being overpowered when they set fire to the dry jungle grass. The wind blew the flames against the attacking party who had to retreat. This let the robbers away again, but the owners still followed pluckily after them till near Suphan when all their exertions were rendered useless.

Some head village men and *amphoes* [district officers] there had the owners arrested on the ground that they were traveling out of their own *Monthon* [region] without passports so were probably thieves themselves. They had perforce to return home again without their cattle, but they have now applied to Bangkok for a warrant to arrest the thieves.

—April 1900

A Siamese from the country bought a revolver in a City pawnshop yesterday and then went to Sampeng where he bought a few cartridges. Having got the cartridges he proceeded to load the revolver when he was promptly arrested by the police and taken to a police station to reflect on the intricacies of the law relating to firearms.

—August 1900

Kadersah, the famous hat snatcher was again before the British Court today on the usual charge. Mr. Black sent him to gaol for three months, remarking that on the next occasion he would be convicted he would be sent to Singapore for two years.

—June 1901

complaints that Chinese criminals deported from 'The Straits' would transit in Bangkok on their way home and, finding easy pickings, would stay.

The principal crimes were burglary and petty theft, bag snatching being the most frequent. It was an open secret in both the Thai and European communities that whenever an item disappeared from one's house, the next day one could go to Nakorn Kasem — known as the 'Thieves' Market' — off New Road, and in most cases retrieve it for a portion of the original cost.

In 1905, the triangle of land wedged between Rajdamnern Avenue and Rajini Road was the site of Lahu Thos jail. That changed in King Vajiravudh's reign and this monument of Mae Phra Toranee — the goddess who wrang water from her hair to drown the demons distracting Buddha in his final meditation to reach Nirvana — was built as a memorial to the King's Royal Mother, Queen Saovabha Bongsri. Since 1882, the land behind the statue has been the site of the Ministry of Justice. The original building, built by a German company, was torn down in 1959 and replaced by a modern structure.

BANGKOK'S RESIDENCES FOR MISCREANTS

Crime was a natural component of the city's life, so there was a need to house criminals to protect society. During the reign of Rama I, a stockade was built opposite the eastern wall of Wat Po. Called the Wat Po Prison, in English, prisoners were incarcerated not in individual cells but in large barracks.

Late in the 19th century, a second jail, Lahu Thos (known to Europeans as Bangkok Jail) was built on the present site of the Mae

Phra Toranee statue, conveniently in front of the Ministry of Justice, itself constructed in 1882. Lahu Tos held defendants awaiting trial and convicts serving terms of less than one year. Prison guards were unsalaried. They were expected to support themselves by using the prisoners as free labor on whatever money-making projects the guards could devise.

In 1892, King Chulalongkorn initiated a series of prison reforms. Recognizing that the system was open to abuse, he abolished the practice of using prison labor and guards became salaried government employees. In 1893, the King sent a delegation of officials to Singapore to study the Old Bailey prison. On their return, he ordered the construction of the Bangkok Central Prison on Mahachai Road. Its most famous resident was Hok Sing, incarcerated there in

Left: Prisoners remained shackled as they worked in this lumber yard, probably to pay their guards' salaries. Right: The buildings haven't changed but their purpose has. This is looking north on Mahachai Road with the Bangkok Central Prison on the left, the city wall and the tram tracks on the right. The prison, built in 1893, was modeled on the Old Bailey jail in Singapore. In 1998, the prison yard was transformed into a beautiful park, and the former cell blocks became administration buildings and a prison museum.

> Six horses were brought up from Singapore the other day for the Police Department. They are strong animals specially selected for drawing the prison vans.
> —April 1900

1927 after he and his henchmen tried to steal the Crown Jewels and robes of Rama VI from the chambers of the Royal Palace.

Hok Sing escaped but was soon recaptured and sent to serve out his term in the new Bang Kwang Prison, built to the north of the city in Nonthaburi in 1930 to hold long-term convicts. Lahu Thos was closed and its inmates were transferred to Bangkok Central Prison, which became a holding center for defendents awaiting trial and for short-term prisoners.

From its inception, Bangkok Central Prison has been a city landmark. Its outer wall was topped by a meter-high lattice of bricks which were not cemented in place. At first glance, the loosely-stacked structure suggested slack security but any escapee grabbing it would inevitably pull it apart, bringing a mass of bricks down with him, and usually injuring himself. Thus, the seemingly slipshod arrangement was in fact a quite effective deterrent to escapes.

In 1996, having outlived its usefulness, Bangkok Central was closed and its precincts were converted into the Rommaneenak Park. The administration building and some cells became a prison museum serving as a reminder of an era when convicts were not treated gently.

Law enforcement was provided by a national police force which in 1904 numbered 3,398 men, 2,679 of them assigned to Bangkok. The force was headed by two Britons, Commissioner of Police, John Lawson, and Superintendent Miller who, supported by 13 Danish officers commanded an eclectic mix of constables comprising nearly 3,000 Thais, Chinese (charged with overseeing affairs in Chinatown), and 320 Indians, Sikhs, and Pathans.

Nearly 700 of the force's men were assigned to the Provincial Gendarmerie which had been created in 1897 and given jurisdiction in Bangkok *monthon* as the administrative precursor of the 'province' was called. In 1904, the provincial police served under the leadership of a Dane, Colonel G. Schau. Over the following decade, the force would expand its numbers and its activities into 15 of Thailand's 21 other *monthon*. Each constable was armed with a Mannlicher magazine carbine, and was given 80 rounds of ammunition a year for practice. Each night, patrols were dispatched to outlying districts where civil officials would hand over any law-breakers they had

The average pawnbroker in Bangkok is always glad to receive stolen goods for he knows he can drive a good bargain. This little weakness of his is so well known that it is sometimes taken advantage of.

On Saturday evening a Siamese rushed up to a Chinese pawnbroker near Talat Noi with a good-sized durian and gasped: "Here, quick! I have just stolen this and the owner will be after me. Give me two *salungs* [50 *stang*], quick quick!"

It was a fine durian worth five or six times the money and the Chinaman passed over the coins, grabbed the fruit and hid it away from the eyes of any possible claimant. In a day or two he brought out the durian and opened it in the hope of enjoying a very fine meal. But the fruit had been eaten already and the only thing the shell contained was mud.

—April 1900

arrested during the day. The suspects would be marched to Bangkok for trial and, if convicted, incarcerated.

While there are no figures for the criminals in the provinces, precise statistics were kept of Bangkok's malefactors. For the year ending March 31, 1908, 18,887 crimes were reported to the authorities. Police nabbed 15,958 persons, and sent 11,185 of them to jail. Assuming Bangkok had a population of 500,000, the number jailed or arrested represents a jail population constituting 2.2 percent of the city's population, not counting convicts incarcerated for longer periods. [13]

In the same year, deaths caused by vehicles were tabulated at 98 persons, of whom 76 died. Twenty-one of the victims were struck by trams, three by motorcars, and the rest were run down by horse-drawn carriages.

A survivor spiffed up in a new coat of paint, one of the ever-present pawnshops that once served as repositories for stolen goods, today acts as a poor man's loan office. This one sits at the Pan Fan end of Larn Luang Road.

RECREATION

In an age before restaurants and the use of hotels as social venues, most entertaining took place at home. During the day, while the men were at work, women paid social calls on each other or gathered for afternoons of playing card games like bridge, cribbage, and whist. Teas were a staple pastime, especially those designed to welcome the newly-arrived or farewell departing members of the community. There were also meetings to discuss the library or support for charity events.

In the evenings, they invited each other to dinner. After dining on a meal comprising several courses, they might play parlor games and sing songs around the piano but more often than not, the men would repair to the parlor to smoke, drink neat whiskies, and talk 'manly' talk, while the women were expected to withdraw elsewhere to talk of things that, according to the men, would only be of interest to other women.

Outside the home, elite Europeans and Thais alike disported themselves at one of Asia's finest race courses, and at several opulent recreational clubs. The United Club had been established in the 1880s, its officials erecting a handsome building at the corner of Siphya Road and New Road. In its high-ceilinged, fan-cooled halls, members could

The Bangkok C.C. has found that cricket is not much of an attraction here except when an outside team visits the port — on a British gunboat as a rule — but the game is not to be forgotten if the City Cricket Club can help it.

This organisation has recently played three matches against a team somewhat vaguely termed 'Shipping' and has proved superior each time. On Saturday afternoon, they beat the Shipping eleven by 64 runs to 49 in the first innings. Going in again, the Shipping had made 30 for the loss of six wickets when the stumps were drawn. Another match was brought off yesterday afternoon when the B.C.C. put on 108 to which the Shipping replied with 78.
—February 1900

King Chulalongkorn, 25 years old when this photo was taken in 1877, relaxes with his brothers, friends, and retainers at a game of croquet on the lawn of the Grand Palace. The lawn later became the forecourt for the Chakrimahaprasad, the building most recognized for its European design topped by three golden spires.

play billiards or cards or, if they felt more energetic, exercise in a gymnasium and swimming pool. The Club overlooked well-tended grounds used for cricket and other field games. It also offered dinners, socials, dances, and lectures to while away the evening hours. Unlike other Bangkok social clubs, the United Club was open to all, regardless of national origin.

> The first of the Cinderella dances of the season will be given at the United Club on the evening of Saturday the 20th inst.
> —October 1900

Most clubs catered to particular nationalities. The Deutscher Klub had been founded in 1890 to serve the German community. The clubhouse of the British Club, established in 1903, still sits off Suriwongse Road near the Dejo Road intersection. Thai nobles formed their own social organization, the Dvi Panya Club, and built their clubhouse in the shady Saranrom Gardens, just east of Wat Phra Kaew.

In 1900, a royal charter was granted to build the Royal Bangkok Sports Club on Henri Dunant Road, named in honor of the Swiss founder of the Red Cross. The RBSC soon became a favored meeting place for socialites and sportsmen, offering members a large race course, a golf course, a cricket pitch, pools, and other sports facilities. It also hosted numerous soirees, social gatherings, and fancy balls. Of all the clubs, only the RBSC and the British Club have survived, and both on their original grounds.

While all the clubs provided sports facilities, not everyone

agreed that strenuous physical exercise was a good idea in the tropics. Skeptics were concerned that physical exertion could adversely affect one's health: "One of the biggest fetishes to which the Britisher especially bows down in the East is exercise. Taken in moderation, such exercise as a round of golf or a set or two of tennis, provided one takes care to avoid chill by changing one's clothing before cooling, is an excellent method of stirring up the liver. The 'muddied oafs' who undergo a couple of hours' violent exercise every afternoon, and an hour of dumb-bells, Indian clubs, or the like, before starting work in the morning, and who seem never to be happy unless in a state of profuse perspiration and absolute fatigue, are more frequently in the

Above: In 1901, King Chulalongkorn granted a royal charter for the establishment of the Royal Bangkok Sports Club and this handsome clubhouse was built soon after. Lower: The RBSC track draws the finest horses in the kingdom to a 10-race card every other weekend except during the rainy season when the track is too slippery. On alternate Sundays, races shift to the cross-town Turf Club. Opposite page, top: The German Club with some of its early members. Bottom: Many of the clubs were quite elegant, decorated in a style that made them seem like European oases in a land far from home.

doctor's hands than even the men who take no physical exercise at all. The greater proportion of them have to be sent home on sick leave, and many of them have their end in the local cemetery. It would seem that they use up all their spare energy in 'recreation' as they call it, and have nothing to fall back upon when they do happen to fall sick. If one would only remember that one is living in a country not suited to Europeans, that a hard day's work is more trying here than at home..." [14]

Of a more cerebral nature was the Engineering Society of Siam, where members discussed technical subjects and arranged outings to observe construction projects. Similarly, the Siam Society, founded in 1904, served as a center for the academic exploration of

Below left and below: Two views of the same intersection taken 10 years apart. The house — and later the branch of Kiam Hoa Heng provisioners — stands at the eastern entrance to Chinatown at the point where Yaowaraj Road meets New Road. In 1900, it was a busy tram stop; today, it is jammed with car traffic. A new addition to the neighborhood is a tall Chinese gate to demarcate the eastern edge of Chinatown. Opposite page, top: Aside from the raintrees than now shelter it, Christ Church on Convent Road looks almost exactly as it did when it was built in 1905.

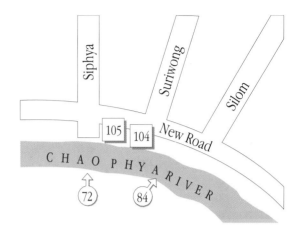

Thailand's archeology, history, art, language and other aspects of culture.

Aside from the magazines that arrived from overseas months out of date, there were few activities to stimulate the mind. The Ladies' Circulating Library had been founded in 1869 to provide the foreign community with English-language books. First housed in private homes, in 1871 the collection was moved to the Protestant Chapel. In 1900, Jenny Neilsen, wife of Dr. Heyward Hays, the Consulting Physician to His Siamese Majesty's Court, arranged for the books to be moved to the New Road home of Mr. T.C. Taylor of the Gold Mines of Siam. The library continued its peripatetic existence, finding a new

Left: In 1900, this handsome building was the Customs House where goods entering Bangkok by river were examined. It is now a police station and although in dilapidated condition, still reflects much of its original elegance.

A postal report from Chiang Mai notes that letters arrive from Bangkok in about three weeks and from London in about six weeks. The London mail comes via Moulmain [in Burma] and Raheng [Tak].

Early in 1899 owing it is said to some departmental dispute in Bangkok, the local post offices in the North were not supplied with stamps and all letters destined for Europe had to be sent to Bangkok to be stamped. This caused much inconvenience and a delay in delivery of about three weeks. Since the visit of the vice-minister of the Interior to the North, the mails have come in very regularly.

The telegraph lines to Moulmain and to Bangkok, also to Lakhon [Lampang], Phrae and Nan are in good working order. Although communication is often interrupted for 10 days at a time, an answer can always be got from Bangkok, distant 450 miles, in three days at most.

But businessmen are thankful even to be able to do that, and to feel somewhat confident that an interruption will not exceed a fortnight.

—November 1900

Below left: Before a new Central Post Office was built on New Road in 1937 on the former site of the British Legation, Bangkok's main post office sat on the riverbank at the foot of the Memorial Bridge. It was torn down in 1982 to make way for the northern approach to the new Phrapoklao Bridge. Below: The latest addition to the Central Post Office, completed in time for the new millennium, the CAT Telcom Tower sports a tall antenna, symbolic of changes in traditional postal communication in the latter half of the 20th century.

AN EVENING ON THE RIVER

The 'Meinam' (river) as the Europeans called the Chao Phya, was an integral part of city life in the 19th and much of the 20th century.

There is so much romance in whatever may be seen by lamplight or moonlight on the Meinam that we may as well go there to-night; as there is no moon this quarter, the artificial lights will appear brighter. Banjore has secured us a *sampan*, and we are soon in pandemonium. Amidst all this commotion, we enjoy the effect of light on the moving water; Aladdin's lamp is reflected from all sides. The floating theatres add glare and glitter; the supernumeraries stand on the platforms, beckoning with their firebrands; others guard the lights of the many-colored paper lanterns; and here is a show where some of the actors stand without, giving tempting examples of the entertainment to be enjoyed within.

Near at hand is a broth and curry and rice shop. Two fellows on a float are striving with stringed instruments to tempt some of the pleasure-seekers to enter and amuse their stomachs. Fruit shops and toddy boats, all with gay lanterns; and beyond, on a floating platform in the subdued light, stands a screen, on which a light from within and behind casts a series of silhouettes. The performer's hands and arms are posed in such a manner as to produce representations of birds, animals, and human beings; many amusing contests between the characters and ludicrous predicaments of mirthsome Judys are thrown on the screen. The object of this amusing entertainment is not so innocent as it appears to be.

The artistic performance of the silhouette-maker is interrupted at intervals by a company of quasi-musicians who, by a terrific blast of horns and ringing of gongs, call on the innocents to try Dame Fortune. These are floating gambling shops, where, at games similar to roulette, so much coin changes hands of an evening that an implement resembling a coal-scoop is used to shovel in the money, the bankers at the same time paying the winning players with their hands, which should give all level heads an idea of the chances in the game.

Maxwell Sommerville, *Siam on the Meinam*, 1897.[15]

The whereabouts of the Siamese theatrical troupe who have been touring Europe for the past six months, have now been discovered. They are in Amsterdam — stranded. It should now be evident that there is no money in European appreciation of the *lakhon* and we fancy it is unlikely that the promoters will respond to the appeal for yet another large sum of money. The wisest course will be to get the troupe brought back to Siam at once. Nai Boosra Mahin and his troupe's lack of success recalls the worse fate of the team of Siamese football players that Mr. Solomon took to Australia in 1890. They were reduced to a frightful state of destitution, one died and the survivors were finally sent back by the authorities in Australia.

—April 1900

home in Chartered Bank Lane in 1903, before shifting to several other establishments. Finally, after Jenny's death in 1920, her husband in 1922 funded the construction of the library's permanent home on Suriwongse Road, which bears their names, Neilsen-Hays.

For evening entertainment of a socially-acceptable nature — by polite society anyway — there were very few alternatives to the clubs and residents' homes. Movies had not yet been introduced, and only occasionally would a traveling troupe arrive to perform European plays. Several theaters offered Thai classical dance and drama; the one belonging to Chao Phya Deveswongwiwat, owner of Ban Moh Palace, was considered to be among the best.

Bangkok is now to have a regular cafe concert of an evening. Mme. Meranda opens the house today in Ban Moh street opposite the Hotel de la Paix. There is a garden and a fine verandah and a musical entertainment will be given every evening.

—February 1900

Below: Aside from the trams running past it, almost nothing of the Chalerm Krung Theater has changed since it opened in 1933. It was considered the most elegant theater of its day, a stage for theatrical productions and movies attended by royalty and ordinary citizens alike. A 1998 renovation restored it to pristine condition. Opposite: An actress in a Thai drama.

Decidedly less savory — and certainly no place for ladies — were the bawdy houses and the gambling halls patronized by the rowdier elements of all nationalities. Most of these half-dozen small casinos were located just outside the Pratu Sam Yot city gate off New Road. Bustling 24 hours a day, these dens of iniquity were patronized by players of all ages and sexes, earning the government a tidy sum in licensing fees. The four most popular games of chance derived from Chinese card games, the favorite being *tua*, a variation of *fan-tan*. Players of all social strata squatted around a circular mat, measuring 30 feet in diameter, staking their fortunes in a no-limit game that might see one gambler tossing a few small coins onto the mat while another punter nonchalantly put down thousands of *ticals*, as the *baht* was then called. After each round, croupiers, renowned for their dexterity, wielded large bamboo rakes to collect losers' bets without disturbing those of the winners, seldom making a mistake, however late the hour. Other punters played cards, rolled dice, or waited for the master of ceremonies to announce the winners of the nightly *huay*, the forerunner

Top: A Thai bar at the turn of the century. Below: Gamblers and card sharps may have changed attire over time but the exuberance of their games is unaltered from yesteryear. Opposite page top: Old friends while away a quiet afternoon time playing maak rukh *or Thai chess.*

of the two-digit lottery also licensed by the government until it initiated a seven-digit lottery and the two-digit form became an underground entertainment still pursued today in the poorer neighborhoods.

Like other illicit activities, gambling was the domain of private individuals or cartels called Nai Arkorn ('Master of Taxes' or, curiously, in English, 'farmers'). In an annual auction, the government 'farmed' out, to the highest bidder, the collection of certain duties — there were farmers for casinos, opium sales, alcohol, and fishing. The government allowed the farmers to devise their own fee structures and collection methods, then sat back to watch the revenues flow in. While initially it was to the government's advantage to accept the highest

> A couple of Europeans, both in an inebriated condition, caused quite a stir at the top of Oriental Avenue last evening. They were showing their affection for one another by a free use of a walking stick and an umbrella.
>
> —August 1900

bids, by early in the century officials had began to recognize that such a laissez-faire system offered too much scope for abuse. As bidders raised their offers to untenable levels in order to beat their competitors, they were forced to practice a no-holds-barred approach to collecting debts, which resulted in ill feeling and even violence. In the early years of the new century, the 'farming' system was abolished and revenue collection was placed directly in the hands of government agents.

About the same time the government began to recognize the detrimental effects its support of gambling was having on the poor. As a result, on April 1, 1906 the last of the provincial licensed gambling houses was closed, at a reported loss of revenue to the government of three million *baht*. Of course, games of chance continued to flourish in the villages. Although illegal, city casinos were allowed to operate for a few more years before they, too, were shut down. The government also took steps to suppress opium use by registering vendors and

smokers and by curtailing the creation of new users. Mercifully, addicts were allowed to continue to chase the dragon but their ranks thinned as smokers grew old and died. In 1957, the government abolished the use of opium.

Sampeng still thrived as the city's 'green light' district. Then — just as now with Patpong, Nana Entertainment Plaza, and Soi Cowboy — Sampeng's bordellos and bars were avoided by respectable gentry. Liquor flowed, brawls erupted; knives, fists, and hard words flew. The newspapers reported frequent calls to the police to quell fights, many between Thai soldiers and policemen, a simmering hostility that has not abated down the decades.

> Mlle. Dolores (Trebeli) owns a set of curiously-carved chessmen made out of the bones of a departed chess enthusiast who bequeathed his skeleton for that purpose.
>
> —August 1901

GETTING AWAY

Journeys outside of Bangkok were limited by the lack of transportation. The railway to Paknam provided the only easy escape from the city's fetid air, allowing holidays in seaside cottages. Hardier souls ventured out to sea, sailing down the coast to a sanitarium at Sri Racha. The bravest voyaged across the open water to Koh Si Chang, Thailand's custom's port, where the climate was so salubrious that King Chulalongkorn built a retreat on the island's southern end.

We find little mention of big game hunting in the foreigner's journals. Safaris into the hinterlands generally took more time than most Europeans had at their disposal, and the killing of animals by the elite was frowned upon by Buddhists. In 1835 a friend of Robert Hunter, the first 19th century European merchant to reside permanently in Bangkok, was reportedly beaten by monks after he shot birds near a monastery. By 1900, however, social mores had changed and newspapers frequently reported on sport hunters traveling north to the marshes around Don Muang (near the present airport) to shoot snipe and other birds, or to the Northeast to hunt bigger game.

With the establishment of the Royal State Railways

Department in 1897, railroads began extending iron tendrils into the provinces. When the 71-km. line to Ayutthaya was completed early in 1897, Their Majesties inaugurated it with a journey north to the former capital. By 1901 the line had been extended northeast to Nakhon Ratchasima (Korat). In 1902 Lopburi was brought on line, and mid-1904 saw the completion of the 150-km. line to Petchburi on the southern peninsula. Until the Rama VI Bridge was completed in 1926 trains left from Bangkok Noi Railway Station on the Thonburi side of the river at the juncture with Klong Bangkok Noi. The new bridge made it much easier for vacationers to take weekend trips to marvel at the tremendous stupa at Nakhon Pathom, a popular excursion frequently mentioned in residents' journals.

Left: Only Rama IV Road supported such a wide range of transportation. From the bottom, we see the canal, then the Paknam Railway tracks, several types of vehicles, and the trams. Here, at Ban That Thong, we see two houses peeking above the low shophouses that by 1999 had grown tall enough to obscure them; yet, 50 years later, the houses are still there. When asked, the owner of the one on the right, said his house was 100 years old. When his claim was challenged, he stiffened and said proudly, "I was born in this house 74 years ago." Right: Hualampong Station in the 1920s.

A contributor who knows a good deal about the railway possibilities of Siam, pointed out yesterday some of the weak points in the railway policy of the country and emphasised the importance of encouraging light railways as feeders of the main line.

With most of what he wrote, we are in entire agreement but we think he is wrong in discouraging the construction of the Chiang Mai line. It will not pay, he argues. Probably that is so; it will not pay for some time but we still believe there is good reason for pushing on the line as speedily as possible...With, say, a light railway from Chiang Mai the line would tap the great plain of Chiang Saen and open up a far wider market for the various produce of that important district. Further, the railway would give Bangkok a better chance of competing for the custom of the caravans that come down from Yunnan.

—June 1901

A MENACE TO SHIPPING

This S.S. Donai is become famous, if not for the quantity of her cargo at least for the 'striking' manner in which she makes her presence felt this side of Bangkolem Point. She is the terror of ship and cargo boat owners, as also of those whose property abuts the Menam [the Chao Phya River].

Her latest escapade occurred last evening. The speed at which she came up the river near the G.B.T.C.'s premises was a sight. Then she dropped anchor nearly opposite the Harbour Office. There was a strong flood tide and instead of bringing up gracefully she tried conclusions with the Harbour Department's wharf. The S.S. Bukettingi which was lying there had her after port bulwark stove in and one of her masts sprung. A Public Works Department launch was sunk and three of the Harbour Master's launches were damaged. Also, the wharf itself was broken down. The damage has been roughly estimated at about Tcs. 12,000.

The Donai is today anchored peacefully in front of the Hongkong Bank.

—August 1901

111

WILD WILD EAST

For urban residents, civilized Thailand ended at the city limits. When we read of the creatures lurking in the surounding jungles, it is easy to understand why.

As a train was passing near Korat the other day, a tiger was seen carrying off a deer that it had killed. The engine driver blew the whistle and the tiger dropped the deer and bolted into the jungle in terror.

—August 1901

Cold winds prevail at Korat and although at times it is terribly hot in the day, it is cool at night. With regard to sport, there is plenty to be had. Teal, wild duck, fowl, snipe and hare are plentiful and the military officers are frequently out and return with good bags. Jackals, too, are in abundance if anyone cares to sit up for them at night. At Klong Phai there are plenty of peafowl. At Pak Chong [near Khao Yai National Park], Mr. Grove of the Railway Police bagged a rhino last month.

—January 1901

Bangplasoi in Chon Buri is excited over a tale about a tiger. It seems that on the 9th instant, a man and his wife and child were walking into the town from their home some 500 *sen* [20 km.] away in the jungle. When they reached Bangplasoi hill the woman disappeared.

She had fallen behind and the man sat down and waited until he began to get alarmed. He went to investigate and found blood leading from the road along a jungle path. That scared him and he cleared out for Bangplasoi with his child as quickly as possible.

Four men who were out hunting rabbits on the hill the next day, startled a tiger close to the very spot where the woman was last seen. The animal roared and then bolted. Since then, the people of Bangplasoi have been afraid to go near the place. Evil-minded people are saying that the lady may have eloped and that the presence of the tiger the next day was only a coincidence.

—February 1900

In 1906 the last spike was driven in the 63-km. line to Baet Riew (the popular name for Chachoengsao), and in the same year the northern line reached Nakhon Sawan. Not until 1921 did the northern line enter Chiang Mai, a delay occasioned in part by the need to blast a 1.35-km. tunnel through the Khun Tan Mountains that separated the upper Chao Phya River basin from the Chiang Mai Valley.

Despite the proliferation of roads within the capital, few

reached into the provinces. Low-lying, soggy land defeated road contractors, and as late as 1920, there were still no major highways reaching farther north than Rangsit, just north of Don Muang. The first real motor road, the Sukhumvit Highway, built in the 1930s, ran south to Paknam and then along the coast to Bang Pakong where cars had to be ferried across the river. From Bang Pakong cars either headed north on an old dirt track to Baet Riew or traveled southeast via Chon Buri, Si Racha, Sattahip, Rayong, and Chanthaburi, before

reaching Trat. Pattaya would not become a full-fledged beach resort until the late 1960s.

In 1911 the first airplane touched down on the grass at the Royal Bangkok Sports Club. The RBSC served as the city's air field until 1914 when a proper airport was opened at Don Muang. As late as the 1950s, however, most foreigners rode a steamship home for their leave, a voyage that often took two months.

Even elderly Thais are unable to locate this 1946 photo,. It looks down on Petchburi Road as it T's into Rajdamri/Rajaprarob Road running from top to the bottom of the picture. In 1960, part of the market at the 'T' would be demolished to build New Petchburi Road. As the comparison shot from the top of the Baiyoke II Tower reveals, the landscape would be transformed, with only a Chulalongkorn University building at the very top of the picture, and Wat Patumawanaram to the right of the lake, along Rama I Road, serviving. Rajaprasong intersection was a grove of trees and the World Trade Center an open field. Of interest, the photographer of the companion shot was higher in the air than the plane pilot when the 1946 picture was taken.

> One evening a short time ago, the Manager of the Paknam Railway was returning to Paknam on a trolley. Near the second bridge out from Bangkok, the trolley bumped into and was stopped by an obstruction on the line. It was dark, of course, but the Manager proceeded to investigate the matter and found the obstruction down the bank washing a bad wound on his head. It was a policeman who had gone to sleep on the line. But even that experience did not teach the P.C. wisdom for he had another collision with the Paknam Railway Co., A day or two ago, the Company's Traffic Superintendent had occasion to call on a policeman at the Bangkok terminus to arrest a noted *nakleng* [gangster] who was obstructing the employees in their work and the policeman flatly refused to effect the arrest. Presumably the *nakleng* was a friend of his. On investigation he was found to be the same policeman as had previously been bumped by the trolley. His days in the force are accordingly at an end and he is now in gaol, doing a month's hard.
>
> —February 1900

LOOKING HOMEWARD AFTER YEARS AWAY

It was inevitable that after long years working in a foreign land that the expatriates' thoughts should turn homeward. Most were in Thailand for a fixed period — often the length of their working lives — with long spells of employment punctuated every few years by an all too brief home leave.

Top left: Laying track on the northern line which would not reach Chiang Mai until the 1920s. Left: The 'Siawa', one of many 1920s steamships that carried Europeans to and from their homes before the inauguration of affordable long-distance air transport in the 1950s.

AN EDITORIAL
    The proposal to make a ship canal across the Isthmus of Kra, has been brought forward on several occasions. Surveys have been undertaken, companies have been formed to take up the preliminary studies. Then silence has fallen on the proposal and the Isthmus of Kra, still inviolate, has sunk into forgetfulness.
    Perhaps the failure of the Panama Canal has loomed in the minds of the capitalists at the crucial psychological moment when a call had to be made for funds. Perhaps powerful foreign influences have been interposed. To cut the Isthmus of Kra is to destroy the prosperous port of Singapore.

—August 1901

Note: The proposal to cut a canal across the Isthmus of Kra in the southern peninsula has been rejected time and again, yet phoenix-like rises periodically to be considered, yet again. Nearly a century after the construction of the Panama Canal — one of the 20th century's most successful ventures — the Kra Canal still has not been built.

While few Europeans ever envisioned retiring here, when the time came to go home to live out their final years, many found themselves surprised that their native lands seemed as alien to them as Thailand had when they first stepped off the boat. Some retirees packed their possessions, looked around at the comfortable lives they had created for themselves, looked at their friends, Thai and foreign...and unpacked their bags, choosing to remain in the city which had become their home.

There is little doubt that many of those who did choose to return home — strangers though they may have become in their native lands after such extended absences — gazed back at Thailand with wistful eyes. In 1904, Wright and Breakspear wrote, "...Certain it is that most Europeans who have once dwelt for any length of time in Bangkok, and have left the town, are generally only too willing to return to it." [16]

Some things never change, no matter how many years pass. A great nostalgia for Bangkok by those who have left it is a curious aspect of the city's elusive charm that remains unaltered today.

HOME LEAVE

Contemporary writers offered advice on the factors that employers should take into consideration when determining home leave and vacations for their expatriate staff:

The question has often been asked how long one should spend in Bangkok before one's first spell of long leave. This naturally depends upon a number of factors, such as the general condition of health, the possibility of being spared from one's duties, and, of course, the state of one's purse. Taking it as a general rule, however, three years for a woman and five years for a man is a long enough period for a first spell, and the period of leave should in either case allow of no less than six months being actually spent in a temperate climate. This practically entails nine months' leave from duty, as to allow of three months' being spent between the home and return journey.

Further periods of work in the tropics, should not extend to more than three years, with six months' leave at the end of such term. Governments, commercial firms, and, in fact, all employers of labour, would find that such a system of work and leave would make for the health and efficiency of their staff, and therefore for economy in the end. It is no economy to train a man in his work for several years, and then be forced to invalid him home for good at the very time when he is becoming a valuable servant.

The question of short leave, say for a month or two, is one which often crops up in a medical man's experience in Bangkok. Perhaps a man has had a mild attack of malarial fever, typhoid fever, congestion of the liver or the like. It may not be necessary to send him home, as all that may be required is a short sea trip or a few weeks in a cool climate. Siam is still, unfortunately, most grievously deficient in hill stations or other health resorts. Srimaharacha [Si Racha] is practically the only local sanatorium, but it is not much of a change...Still better will be Chiengmai and the hills beyond when the present railway has been extended so far. Further afield we have Singapore, the return trip to which will often set one upon one's feet again. Then we have Hongkong from October until the end of March; Japan during the spring and autumn; Java during July, August, and September; Pinang Hill during the northeast monsoon; Kandy and Nuwara Eliya in Ceylon from December to April; and Ootacamund, on the Nilgiri Hills, from April till October.

—Wright & Breakspear, *Twentieth Century Impressions of Siam*. [17]

Bangkok on the Cusp of the Third Millennium

Thirty five years ago there were no streets in Bangkok. All traffic was carried on by boats. Numerous canals still compete with the street traffic. At late as 10 years ago, there were no more than nine miles of paved streets in the whole city. Today, there are over 47 miles and many new streets are being opened up each year. Moreover, the old iron and wooden bridges are being replaced by modern steel bridges.

The King himself builds one steel bridge each year out of his private funds as a gift to the city and this is opened to the public with some ceremony on his birthday. Seventy-five miles of canals traverse the city of Bangkok, a large percentage of which has been added in recent years. The tendency, however, is to make streets instead. Outside of the city and extending all over the vast alluvial plain of Siam are a great number of canals, hundreds of miles in extent which serve as the highways of the country. These canals have all been dug within the last 50 years and up to 10 years ago were the only means of communication except by paths through the jungle.

The opening up of rich rice fields is giving a new aspect to the question of agriculture in this country. Besides the thousands who are taking up small holdings, there are also those who are buying large estates to await an increase in values for the cultivation of rice on an extensive scale.

Already the question of better methods and tools for the cultivation of the land is of importance. The crude wheels run by the human foot, the wooden plow with its iron shoe, the wooden-toothed buffalo rake used for a harrow, the scattering of the seed by hand, the thrashing floor of hardened mud and buffalo dung trampled by buffalo hoofs and the winnowing of grain by the shovel and the wind must soon give way to the windmill pump, the steel plows, the improved harrow, the seed drill, and the thrashing machine.

Nothing has been done in these directions for instruments adapted to the peculiar demands of the soil have not yet been invented. Some enterprising American should certainly be able to make agricultural implements suitable for this country and reap substantial financial benefits therefrom.

—Hamilton King, *American Consul-General*, June 1900. [18]

Left: Bangkok's skyline looking southeast from the crest of the Golden Mount with the roofs of the monks' quarters at Wat Saket in the courtyard below.

BANGKOK 2000

From even a cursory reading of the *Times*, it is clear that life in Bangkok a hundred years ago, far from being simple and idyllic, was as chaotic as it is today. It is curiously reassuring to read the dusty stories and realize that despite ten decades and radical alterations in the landscape, little has changed at a human level. Thus, in the newspaper pages, we read not of a dead past but a precursor of our own lives.

Bangkok had great hope for the future. In 1927, Erik Seidenfaden wrote in his *Guide to Bangkok with Notes on Siam*, "the future will see Bangkok as a vast well laid-out, park-like town intersected with a network of broad shady roads running in all directions...In the future when the road from Bangkok reaches Paknam, this place will become another suburb of the capital as the new road will be quickly lined with houses and residences of people who seek to get away from the capital out to the cool breezes of the sea." Seidenfaden was describing Sukhumvit Road. [19]

How has Bangkok met Seidenfaden's expectations? At the

beginning of the third millennium it is a variegated city of eight million people (10 million by unofficial estimates) with the old and the new interlarded. Stand the city on its edge with the eastern end uppermost and it resembles a rich archeological site. Burrow downward from the suburbs, and end at a bottom layer of brilliant monuments of the old royal city that hugs the riverbank.

The city is also jumbled horizontally. Around the middle of the century, owners of mansions with spacious lawns began to construct rows of shops along the streets bounding their properties, with the result that utilitarian modern shophouses often veil elegant old

Opposite page: 'Saphan Han' lay on Sampeng Lane where it crossed Klong Ong Ang just east of Pahurat Road. Its name (Saphan means bridge; Han means pivoting) referred to the original narrow wooden walkway that could be pivoted on a midstream support to let large boats pass. The pivoting bridge was replaced by a fixed span in the reign of King Rama II (1809-1824). It was widened in the reign of King Mongkut (1851-1868), and small shops were built the length of both sides, reminiscent of the Ponte Vecchio in Florence. Those shops were removed in the 1950s and the rather ordinary bridge — with makeshift vendor stalls still lining it — was constructed. Right, New and old: The Baiyoke II Tower — the world's tallest hotel — near Pratunam (top). A bit of history in a quiet lane off Songwat Road (bottom).

THE NEW CENTURY
The Astronomer Royal writes from Greenwich Observatory: The twentieth century begins on January 1, 1901. It has been generally agreed to call the first day of the Christian era A.D. 1, not A.D. "0" and consequently the second century begins with A.D. 101, a hundred years after the beginning of the first year, and so on for succeeding centuries.
The Archbishop of Canterbury, Dr. Adler, the Chinese Ambassador, and Sir Walter Besant take the same view. On the other hand, Sir H.H. Fowler, M.P., President of the Statistical Society writes: "I am of opinion that the twentieth century begins on January 1, 1900." Dr. Parker, in his characteristic way says: "I know the twentieth century begins on January 1, 1900 and no man in his senses can doubt it."
—February 1900

homes hidden behind them. Peering down from the tops of tall buildings — just as when one peeks between shophouses — often reveals small, charming pockets of the past concealed by surrounding structures.

The city skyline has changed dramatically, with sacred spires dwarfed by the secular towers of commerce. Look east from the top of the Golden Mount across the rooftops of the old city and see a jagged mountain range of skyscrapers, a transformation reflecting a philosophical shift in values. But, despite scores of tall buildings — the 94-story, 309-meter tall, Baiyoke II Tower being the tallest — most of Bangkok remains a town of two- and three-story shophouses with family businesses on the ground floor and living quarters upstairs. While stand-alone homes with yards have largely disappeared from the city center — victims of a manic real estate market in the 1990s — the edge of the city has spawned bucolic housing estates ranged around golf courses, the most striking new use for land.

> We are still talking of the approaching railway communication from this town with the outer world which must come about. From Martaban, the line will join the Burma railway at or near Pegu. From Moulmein eastwards, it is the only feasible route for a railway to Bangkok.
>
> Moulmein will be the terminus at the north of the great Malay railway that will connect Singapore one day, linking up with other lines (more than half of which are already built) to create a line running all the way to London.
>
> —August 1900
>
> Note: Bangkok is still waiting for the line to London to be completed.

Just as the end of the last century witnessed a shift from wood to concrete as the preferred building material, the past decade has seen glass and metal in a variety of hues supplanting concrete. Gleaming surfaces of silicone, chrome, and anodized aluminum brazenly shout out the city's new prosperity.

One of the city's most salient changes has been the slow but relentless transition from agrarian to industrial. Cows, which even a decade ago roamed the back lanes of Sukhumvit Road, have all but disappeared. On city streets, one occasionally sees elephants, but they have been turned into beggars by deforestation in Thailand's Northeast. For housekeepers, a noticeable change has been the disappearance of fresh markets from the city's core, and the rise of supermarkets in their stead. Small family-owned groceries are also

vanishing, replaced by flashier convenience stores operating 24 hours a day.

The most dramatic changes have come at the century's end. Expressways and tollways slash through old neighborhoods transforming Bangkok from a city where houses were paramount to one where the automobile rules. Expressways might have marginally speeded the flow of traffic, but they have most certainly altered the

city's aesthetics; roadways 20 and 30 meters high dominate the view down most streets. Impressive they are; beautiful, they are not.

And after decades of discussion, Bangkok is finally to enter the new millennium on its long-awaited Skytrain monorail whose two lines run from Moh Chit (opposite Chatuchak Weekend Market) to the Sathorn Bridge and from the National Stadium to Soi 81, a half kilometer past Phrakanong Canal on Sukhumvit Road. Shortly into the new century, Bangkokians will dive below ground on a new subway system. The pillars for the skytrain have turned hallowed streets into veritable tunnels, but, we are told, efficiency and economy — the new determinants of development — decree their necessity.

Some things have not changed. One still cannot drink the waters of the Chao Phya, most canals are putrid, and Bangkok still floods each rainy season. And, despite the promise of salvation by

Left: The vegetable gardens may have been cemented over but despite the passage of 50 years, Ploenchit and Wireless roads are still filled with trees. And in this view from Petchburi looking south the flagpole still rises high above the British Embassy at middle right.

Timber for ordinary buildings is dear at present, a fact which renders the public rather more attentive to the voice of the professional forester than it generally is. The figures and areas dealt with by experts in this art are generally so large that they are looked on as rather outside the range of practical business.

But the shrinkage of the world is bringing all its 'timber properties' into reach. Their sites, boundaries and contents are all well known with one notable exception: that of the great tropical forest which belts the globe. All nations and languages — the civilised ones, that is to say, for the savage, like the peasant, is always the enemy of trees — are beginning to take stock both of the waste and extravagance of the past and of the principal left for the future.

—May 1901

elevated roadways, traffic jams remain world class, seeming to worsen with each passing year. Gridlock has become such a fact of life that few bother to mention it except as a perfect excuse for turning up late for an appointment. Noise, pollution, all the dementia and detritus spawned by a modern metropolis have in Bangkok outstripped the infrastructure's ability to cope, like a pubescent boy constantly outgrowing new sets of clothes.

On the positive side, we have air-conditioners, and we don't worry about dying from communicable diseases. There are more leisure activities, better access to overseas news, and it is easier to get out of town and to foreign countries (and we no longer need four months of travel time for home leave). And there is the hope that Bangkok will have its first complete sewage system not too far into the new century.

Also on the bright side, more and more, citizens are talking

Two contrasting views of Bangkok's future. Left: A concrete tunnel beneath the Skytrain on Rama I Road. Right: A corridor of greenery along Prachan Road just outside the southern wall of Thammasat University.

about improving the quality of life and preserving the past. Recent changes are small but encouraging. Many streets are now green corridors of sizeable trees; planted by the municipality, they are maintained by citizens. The city is also reclaiming some of its rural heritage by creating parks, not just big showcase parks but also small neighborhood parks.

Economic and ecological necessities coupled with an increasingly educated and vocal populace will dictate a more rational approach to city planning, and a demand for an enhanced quality of life. Given the automobile's value as a status symbol, we will probably

Right: The grimness of gridlock, a feature of daily life for the city commuter, and a dilemma only marginally improved by the construction of expressways and mass rapid transit systems, above and below ground.

EDITORIAL

It is Christmas again, the last Christmas of the century and the thoughts of the whole Christian world turn once more to the solemn aspiration for 'Peace on Earth and Goodwill towards Men!'

But the century is ending as it began, and though men must think of the ideal for the moment, they cannot avoid the irony of the contrast between what they pray for and the situation that they have created today. Nations as individuals pray for peace and shape their policies sincerely enough, but good intentions may on occasion pave the way to an undesirable place. And while we sing of peace on earth at this Christmastide, it is war that is in our minds and the possibility of further wars.

All the great Powers have troops in China and the agreement on a joint Note that has at last been arrived at is but one more in a game that is of vital importance to the world but of which no one can foresee the outcome. And, just as at last Christmas, reinforcements are being hurried out to South Africa to deal with the somewhat grave situation that has arisen there. The end of the Boer war will evidently require a further strong effort on the part of the British Empire.

—December 1900

GRAPPLING WITH JAMS

Bangkok residents at both ends of the 20th century grumbled about the city's traffic jams. Here, J.T. Jones, who had already lived in the capital for two years, reveals his frustration with getting from one end of town to the other by boat:

"One of the most annoying and grievous circumstances attending the accomplishment of any business in this country, is the delay incident to traveling even from one part of Bangkok to another. Whenever a person wishes to transact any business a mile distant which, at home, would easily be done in an hour, it will ordinarily require three or four here. He is altogether dependent on his boat. His boatmen are to be called, his boat unlocked (should it be left unlocked, or exposed it is almost sure to be stolen. I have had three stolen, one of them while fastened by an iron chain and padlock), baled out, his mat spread, and his boat brought to a convenient landing place (if he can find any).

By this time, more than half an hour is consumed. If the tide opposes him, he cannot generally go more than two miles an hour; and if the tide favors one way, it must usually oppose him the other. When he reaches his destination, it is usually among a fleet of boats — and it is not till after much jostling and some danger that he can get safely landed, and then it is more probable than otherwise, during a great part of the year, that he will be landed in the mud, or water ankle deep. Tho' the expenses of this mode of traveling are heavy, and the other disadvantages numerous, the loss of time and exposure to the sun are most to be deplored."

—J.T. Jones. January 6, 1836. [20]

not soon see the elimination of cars in favor of public transportation, but with more stringent emission controls — perhaps even the introduction of electrical or solar-powered vehicles — Bangkok may revert to the city it was in 1900, with cleaner air. Were such changes instituted, would the citizenry not be astounded by how quiet — and how uncrowded — the city would seem?

Hopefully, once again the rivers and canals will flow with clean water as a result of a sewage system which treats wastewater before it enters the waterways. Perhaps there will be a resurgence of life on the rivers when and if it becomes possible to swim in them. Aesthetic considerations may even dictate the construction of riverside promenades, re-establishing the river as an integral part of the city rather than as an unwelcome relic of the past to be walled off and ignored.

Bangkok may lose its preeminence as a primate city as Thailand's neighbors open their doors to free trade, creating economic incentives for industry to locate near border-crossings. Perhaps the ASEAN countries and the Greater Mekong Sub-region will come to resemble the European Community, a borderless commonwealth where citizens and goods flow freely back and forth.

Improvements to the transportation and communications systems might possibly promote the city's return to its former spaciousness as its citizens move to the suburbs, a process that has already begun. Both a growing middle class and tele-commuting will accelerate such a migration to the countryside. Without a huge populace to house and support at the core, the more than two million rural laborers who now work in the city may find it more attractive to return to their villages and small towns, further reducing Bangkok's numbers and the demands on its infrastructure.

Some things, however, may never change. Complaints about vendor-crowded sidewalks ring as true today as they did in 1904. Can we realistically ever expect to see the sidewalks cleared of vendors, as municipal authorities have tried for decades? On the other hand, would want to, given the liveliness and human flavor they lend to city streets, a vibrancy not found in shopping malls?

Left: Omnipresent vendors crowd the sidewalks of key Bangkok streets. Top right: Monks in the shadow of the city wall along Mahachai Road. Right: The Mahakan watchtower at Mahachai and Rajdamnern stands as a silent sentinel amidst the onslaught of cars, helpless to stem their flow as it did the invaders at the city's gates early in the 19th century.

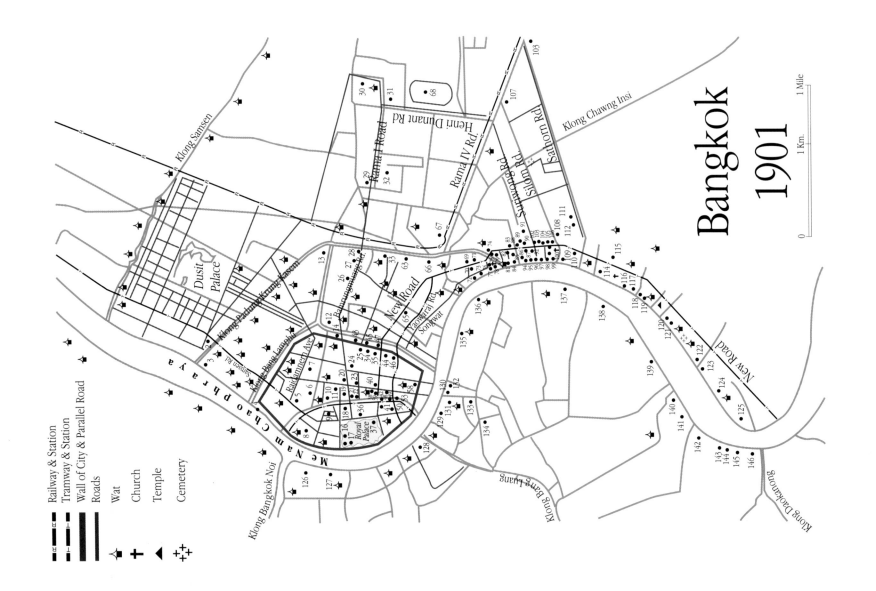

Bangkok
1901

Railway & Station
Tramway & Station
Wall of City & Parallel Road
Roads
Wat
Church
Temple
Cemetery

Me Nam Chao Phraya

Dusit Palace

Royal Palace

New Road

Rama IV Rd.
Rama Road
Henri Dunant Rd.
Surawong Rd.
Silom Rd.
Sathorn Rd.
Klong Chawng Insi
Klong Samsen
Klong Padung Krung Kasem
Klong Bangkok Noi
Klong Bang Lamphu
Samsen Rd.
Mahachai Rd.
Bamrungmuang Rd.
Ratchadamnem Ave.
Yaowarat Rd.
Songwat
Klong Bang Luang
Klong Daokanong

1 Mile
1 Km.

BANGKOK 1901

This 1901 map from the National Archives only hints at how the city looked. For example, it shows no landmarks, and a large portion of the undifferentiated open areas was fields and farms. Nonetheless, it is testament to a city rapidly expanding its boundaries to the east and north. It is also clear that canal development kept pace with road construction, since the waterways were still regarded as important aids to transportation, flood control, and irrigation for the market gardens that now lie beneath tall buildings. The spellings are as they appeared on the original map.

1. Prince Mahit
2. Prince Ratburi
3. Prince Kitia Kawn
4. Prince Nares
5. Prince Kosit
6. Prince Pi San
7. Tukdin
8. Museum
9. Siamese Court
10. Prince Sum Pra Sat
11. Prince Nara
12. Golden Mount
13. Prince Nakawn Chaisi
14. Police Station
15. Foreign Office
16. Treasury
17. Mint
18. War Department
19. Prince Photaret
20. Post Branch
21. Messrs. Badman
22. Local Government
23. Prince Tisseman
24. Prince Wattana
25. School
26. Children's Home
27. Printing Office
28. Phraya Sri
29. Prince Sawasti
30. Lotus Gardens
31. Rifle Range
32. Royal Survey School
33. Hospital
34. Gaol
35. Police Station
36. Royal Garden
37. Artillery
38. Seekak Dispensary
39. Out Fitting Co.
40. American Import Co

41. British Dispensary
42. School
43. Prince Damrong
44. Prince Pichit
45. Boripah Hospital
46. Prince Ong-Noi
47. Boy's English School
48. Police Station
49. Chao Phraya Thwed
50. Garden
51. Ta Tien
52. Police Station
53. John Sampson
54. Royal Survey Office
55. Sunandalaya
56. B. Grimm & Co.
57. Survey Department
58. Siam Electricity Co.,
59. Flag Staff
60. Russian and Danish Consulates
61. Post Office No. 1
62. German Siam Trading
63. Siam Canals, Land and Irrigation Co.
64. Royal Railway
65. Photo Studio
66. Police Station
67. Railway Workshops
68. Race Course
69. Photo Studio
70. Western Dispensary
71. Borsipa Court
72. Public Works
73. Convent
74. Japanese Legation
75. Nai Lert
76. Kian Hoa Heng
77. Messrs. Markwald
78. Austrian Consulate

79. Bangkok United Club
80. Bangkok Times
81. Hong Kong Shanghai Bank
82. Printing Office, Gotte & Co.,
83. Ch. Kinder
84. Oriental Inn
85. Portuguese Consulate
86. British Consulate
87. American Consulate
88. Bangkok Library
89. Italian Hotel
90. Kerr & Co.
91. German Club
92. Police Station
93. Siam Free Press
94. Custom House
95. Post Office No. 2
96. French Consulate
97. Chartered Bank
98. Oriental Hotel
99. East Asiatic Co.
100. Assumption College
101. Siam Observer
102. British Dispensary
103. Bodega Hotel
104. Banque de l'Indo Chine
105. English Pharmacy
106. Bangkok Dispensary
107. Phraya Surisak
108. Hospital
109. Messrs. Howarth Erskine
110. Market
111. Italian Consulate
112. German Consulate
113. German Minister

114. Bangkok Dock Co.
115. Police Station
116. Borneo Co.
117. Messrs. Windsor
118. Consulate for Norway and Sweden
119. Messrs. Markwald
120. Law Sai Seng
121. Bangkok Rice Mills
122. East Asiatic Co.'s Mills
123. Borneo Co.'s Mills
124. Messrs. Clarke Co.
125. S.J. Smith
126. Wang Lang Hospital
127. Royal Dockyard
128. Palace of Late Prince Awng Yai
129. Chao Phraya Bhaskarawongse
130. Praya Bhanuwongse
131. Phraya Chantabun
132. Phraya Montri
133. King's College
134. Chao Phraya Suriwongse
135. River Police Station
136. Lunatic Asylum
137. Pu Huat
138. Deny Mott & Dickson
139. Phraya Samut
140. Bombay Burma T.C.
141. Hok Fok
142. American Mission
143. Arracan Co.
144. Chasua Luan
145. Phraya Swat
146. Hong Seng

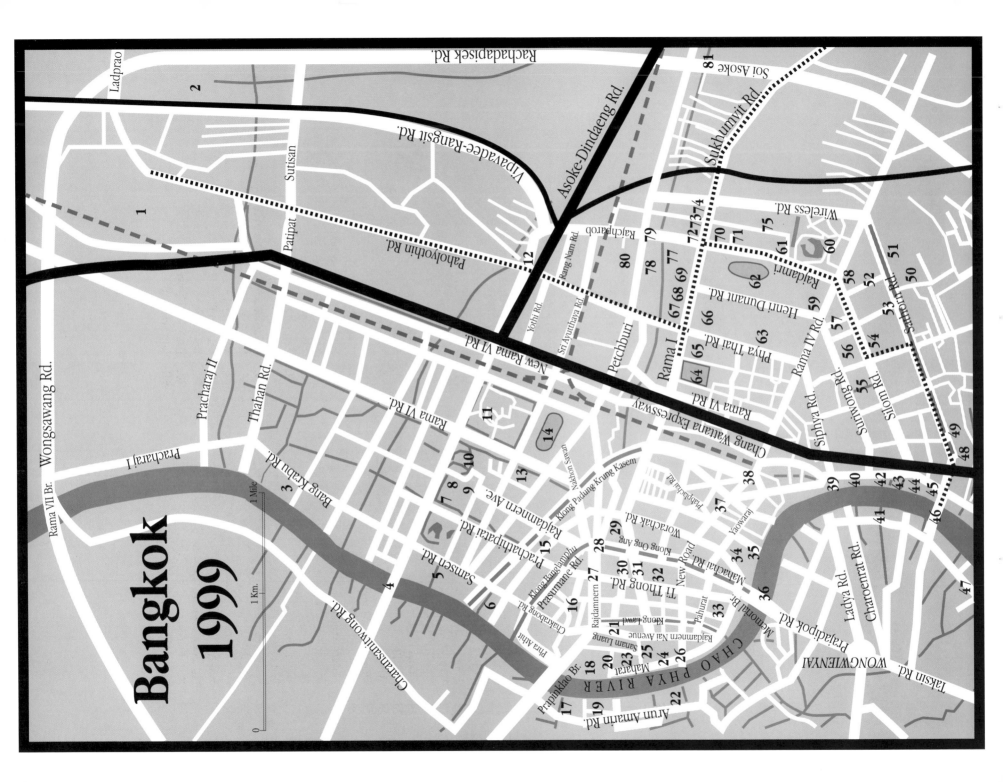

BANGKOK 1999

Apparent in this map is the dramatic expansion of the city's boundaries. The number of new buildings and companies is so extensive that only a few have been included, primarily as referential indicators. Instead, the map is intended to convey a sense Bangkok's new urban boundaries and the physical changes wrought by the construction of a transportation infrastructure.

1. Chatuchak Park
2. Thai Airways International
3. Boonrawd Brewery
4. Krung Thon Bridge
5. National Library
6. Bank of Thailand
7. Vimarn Mek Palace
8. Parliament
9. Ananda Sankhom (Old Parliament)
10. Dusit Zoo
11. Chitrlada Palace
12. Victory Monument
13. Wat Benjamabophit
14. Turf Club
15. ESCAP
16. Wat Bovornivet
17. Bangkok Noi Railway Station
18. National Theater
19. Siriraj Hospital
20. Thammasat University
21. Mae Toranee Statue
22. Wat Arun
23. Silpakorn University
24. Grand Palace
25. Wat Phra Kaew
26. Wat Po
27. Democracy Monument
28. Pan Fah
29. Golden Mount
30. Bangkok Municipality
31. Giant Swing
32. Wat Suthat
33. Pahurat
34. Sampeng Lane
35. Wat Rajburana (Wat Lieb)
36. Phra Pokklao Bridge
37. Wat Mangkorn
38. Hualampong Railway Station
39. Royal Orchid Sheraton Hotel
40. Central Post Office
41. Peninsula Hotel

42. Oriental Hotel
43. East Asiatic company
44. Assumption College
45. Shangri-la Hotel
46. Taksin Bridge
47. Marriott Royal Garden Riverside Hotel
48. Thai CC Tower
49. Bank of Asia
50. Immigration Department
51. Sukhothai Hotel
52. TISCO Tower
53. Anglican Church
54. CP Tower
55. British Club
56. Patpong Road
57. Pan Pacific Hotel
58. .Dusit Thani Hotel
59. Chulalongkorn Hospital
60. Lumpini Park
61. Regent House
62. Royal Bangkok Sports Club
63. Chulalongkorn University
64. National Stadium
65. Mahboonkrong
66. Siam Square
67. Discovery Center
68. Siam Center
69. Wat Pathumawanaram
70. Rajprasong Intersection
71. Regent of Bangkok Hotel
72. Telephone Organization
73. Central Department Store
74. British Embassy
75. Stock Exchange of Thailand
76. U.S. Embassy
77. World Trade Center
78. Panthip Plaza
79. Pratunam
80. Baiyoke II Tower
81. Japanese Embassy

FOOTNOTES

1. Cecil A. Carter, *The Kingdom of Siam, 1904*. New York: G.P. Putnam's Sons, 1904. Reprinted Bangkok: Siam Society, 1988. pp. 107-108.

2. Erik Seidenfaden, *Guide to Bangkok with Notes on Siam*. Bangkok: Royal State Railway Department of Siam, 1927. p. 90.

3. Arnold Wright, Oliver T. Breakspear, *Twentieth Century Impressions of Siam*. London: Lloyd's Greater Britain Publishing Company, 1903 and 1908. Reprinted Bangkok: White Lotus Co. Ltd., 1994. p. 291.

4. Ibid. p. 244.

5. Ibid. p. 244.

6. Kanchanakkhaphan. 'Muang Boron', Vol. 6, Aug.-Nov. 1980.

7. Op cit. Carter. p. 118.

8. J.G.D. Campbell, *Siam in the Twentieth Century: Being the Experiences and Impressions of a British Official*. London: Edward Arnold, 1904. p. 53, 56-57.

9. Op cit. Wright and Breakspear. p. 295.

10. Maxwell Sommerville, *Siam on the Meinam*. London: Sampson Low, Marston, and Company, 1897. Reprinted Bangkok: White Lotus, 1985. p. 21.

11. Op cit. Wright and Breakspear. p. 132.

12. Op cit. Wright and Breakspear. p. 130.

13. Op cit. Wright and Breakspear. p. 110.

14. Op cit. Wright and Breakspear. p. 131.

15. Op cit. Sommerville. pp. 52-53.

16. Op cit. Wright and Breakspear. p. 248.

17. Op cit. Wright and Breakspear. p. 131.

18. Hamilton King, 'Bangkok Times', June 1900.

19. Op cit. Seidenfaden. p. 90.

20. Terwiel, B.J. *Through Travellers' Eyes: An Approach to Early Nineteenth Century Thai History*. Bangkok: Editions Duang Kamol, 1989. p. 204.

BIBLIOGRAPHY

Anonymous. *An Englishman's Siamese Journals 1890-1893*. Reprinted from the Report of a Survey in Siam for private circulation. Bangkok: Siam Media International Books. [no publication date]

Antonio, J. *The 1904 Traveller's Guide to Bangkok and Siam*. Bangkok: Siam Observer Press, 1904. Reprinted Bangkok: White Lotus, 1997.

Campbell, J.G.D. *Siam in the Twentieth Century: Being the Experiences and Impressions of a British Official*. London: Edward Arnold, 1904.

Carter, A. Cecil. *The Kingdom of Siam, 1904*. New York: G.P. Putnam's Sons, 1904. Reprinted Bangkok: Siam Society, 1988.

Chai Ruangsilp. *Prawatsat Thai Samai 2325-2453 Dan Settakit*. Bangkok: Mooniti Krongkanthamara Sangkom Sat Le Manutsaiyasat, Thai Wattana Phanit, 2522.

Chai Ruangsilp. *Prawatsat Thai Samai 2325-2453 Dan Sankhom*. Bangkok: Mooniti Krongkanthamara Sangkom Sat Le Manutsaiyasat, Thai Wattana Phanit, 2519.

Directory for Bangkok and Siam for 1894. Bangkok: *Bangkok Times*, 1894. Reprinted Bangkok: White Lotus, 1996.

The Dynastic Chronicles; Bangkok Era, The First Reign. Chaophraya Thiphakorawong Edition. Translated and Edited by Thadeus and Chadin Flood. Vol. One. Tokyo: The Centre for East Asian Cultural Studies, 1978.

Seidenfaden, Erik. *Guide to Bangkok with Notes on Siam*. Bangkok: Royal State Railway Department of Siam, 1927.

Smith, Malcolm. *A Physician at the Court of Siam*. Kuala Lumpur: Oxford in Asia, 1982.

Smyth, H. Warrington Smyth. *Five Years in Siam; From 1891-1896*. New York: Charles Scribner's Sons, 1898. Reprinted Bangkok: White Lotus, 1994.

Sommerville, Maxwell. *Siam on the Meinam*. London: Sampson Low, Marston & Company, 1897. Reprinted Bangkok: White Lotus, 1985.

Sternstein, Larry. *Portrait of Bangkok*. Bangkok: Bangkok Metropolitan Administration, 1982.

Thompson, P.A. *Siam: An Account of the Country and the People*. 1910. Reprinted Bangkok: White Orchid Press, 1987.

Terwiel, B.J. *Through Travellers' Eyes: An Approach to Early Nineteenth Century Thai History*. Bangkok: Editions Duang Kamol, 1989.

Wright, Arnold, and Breakspear, Oliver T. *Twentieth Century Impressions of Siam*. London: Lloyd's Greater Britain Publishing Company, 1903 and 1908. Reprinted Bangkok: White Lotus, 1994.

PHOTO CREDITS

All black and white photographs are from the author's personal collection or from the National Archives, National Library, Bangkok. All color photographs were taken by the author.

วัดระฆังโฆษิตาราม

กรมแผนที่ทหารสำรวจ
เมื่อสมัยรัชกาลปัจจุบัน

ประทวน...
ช่วงในบรรจบวรราณ

ประตูชนะอีสาน

พระบรมมหาราชวัง

ประตูศรีสุนทร

พระอุโบสถมหาปราสาท

ประตูศักราชโชค
ท่าราชวรดิษฐ์

ป้อมมหาโลหะ
ป้อมไพศพศิล

ประตูนครสินทร

ประตูทักษา

ป้อมสัตบรรพต

พระที่นั่งจักรีมหาปราสาท

วัดพระศรีรัตนศาสดาราม

วัดเทพศิรินทราวาส
สมเด็จพระบรมปิตุ...

ทะเลศาสตรายุทธ

ป้อมขันเงินเพชร
ประตูสวัสดิโสภา

ป้อมสัญชัยใจ
โรงเรีย...

ป้อมสิงขรขัณฑ์
ป้อมชัยชนะยุท

ป้อมฤทธิรุดโรมรัน

ป้อมอนันตคิ...

ประก...
กรมทหารบก...

ศาลตราชูวัตร์